Dread and the Dead Filled the Dunnam House

By
Doris "Dusty" Smith

PublishAmerica
Baltimore

First printing

At the specific preference of the author, PublishAmerica allowed this work to remain exactly as the author intended, verbatim, without editorial input.

ISBN: 1-4137-9837-3
PUBLISHED BY PUBLISHAMERICA, LLLP
www.publishamerica.com
Baltimore

Printed in the United States of America

This book is dedicated to the **Dunnam family** for enduring a year of utter hell and surviving it. To **Edd Dunnam** for his perseverance and dedication to his family and their safety. **To Beth Dunnam** for her hope, kindness and hard work to keep her family together. And to **Emily Dunnam** for being the bravest little girl I have ever met.

To **Troy Taylor, Dave Juliano** and **Kelly Weaver** for all of their guidance, support, help and time. Thanks for listening, advising and being there.

To my Mother, **Marge Rovegno;** I am glad you are beginning to realize that I am not crazy and really enjoy the work I do. There is a need in this world for all belief systems and none of them are right for everyone. I am glad you found yours and now allow me the right to enjoy mine.

Special thanks to **Mark Barfield** and his wonderful editing skills

And last but not least, love and hugs and thanks to my cousin **Roger Scott** for designing my book cover!

Table of Contents:

Chapter One:
Initial Contact

Strange things always seemed to surround my life. Maybe it's my Karma, maybe it's fate. I don't really know. And no longer care to know. I have learned to live with it over the years. Nothing I had experienced or dealt with to this point in my life could have prepared me for what I was about to be faced with.

It was the end of September 2001. We all had much to deal with after the terrorist attack on the World Trade Center, the heroes who crashed the plane in Pennsylvania and the attack on the Pentagon. The lives that were lost, the new fears we all now faced, the numbness we all felt. I felt it would be improper to advertise for cases to work in the wake of it all. Ghost hunting is not something many are open to, and with the massive changes we all now faced, I felt I should keep a lower profile, so to speak. I began searching the Internet for more obscure places to post information about the research group. I found one such place on an AOL message board. In preparation for the upcoming Halloween season, AOL had put up a message board asking people to post information about haunted places in my area. This was great, I thought. Free advertising and in a place asking for it! Little did I know at the time the response I would get from such an obscure listing.

A few days after posting, I received an email from Edd Dunnam. At first I thought it might be a joke. After reading it over for the third time, I realized it was not. Edd's spelling, grammar and punctuation were a bit rough to get through initially. After meeting and getting to know him, he readily admits this flaw. His email explained some "strange" occurrences taking place in the house he, his wife and children lived in. He further stated his wife Beth was pregnant. Edd wrote even their daughter Emily, 18 months old, was affected by these occurrences. And his two boys who visited on weekends had also commented on odd experiences in the house. They were becoming afraid to stay at Dad's new house, he wrote. Edd explained they were renting the house and the owner also had problems in the house which Edd would tell me about later. He repeated several times in the email he was not a lunatic, but was starting to feel like one. He needed some help in dealing with all that was going on…to keep his sanity and his family together and safe.

One thing I have learned in doing this kind of research is when someone starts out by telling you you'll think they're crazy, you usually have a solid case to work. Nothing could have been truer were the Dunnam house was concerned. This is the type of case every ghost hunter dreams they could have…until they actually get it. I've been told by many fellow researchers and so-called authorities in the field this was my "Superbowl case."

I printed out the email and shared it with some of the core members of my research group, Daytona Beach Paranormal Research Group, Inc. I must admit we were all quite excited about being able to work a case with this much purported activity. Edd wrote he was awakened suddenly one night by the smell of smoke in the house. He quickly jumped from his bed in his "birthday suit" to race out the door into the hallway, yelling back at Beth to get up. As he looked into his sons' bedroom on his way to grab his daughter, he pushed open the door and what he saw made caused him to stop dead in his tracks. On the end of his youngest son's bed he wrote he saw a man sitting with his head in his hands.

Being a former Army Ranger, Edd wrote his survival skills went on automatic and he instantly took a martial arts stance, ready to fight the intruder in his home. He stared the intruder down while screaming obscenities at him. He yelled back across the hall to Beth, "Get out of here, now!" Realizing his "John Henry" was still flying in the breeze, he paused for a moment in embarrassment but when he looked back up, the man on the end of the bed had vanished. The smell of the cigar smoke still lingered heavily in the room as Edd ran back across the hall to get his wife Beth.

Edd continued that when Beth entered the room she said she could also smell the heavy odor of cigar smoke in the room and the said room felt "like it was freezing." They checked on the sleeping boys and then went to check on their infant daughter. All the children were sound asleep. They checked the house for any signs of an intruder or fire and found nothing. When Edd and Beth returned to their own bedroom, Edd told Beth what he'd seen before she joined him.

After he finished, Beth said that just a few days before, she woke up suddenly to find an older woman dressed in a housecoat standing in the bathroom doorway staring at her. Beth said she lay there for a moment trying to wake up to make sure she was actually seeing what she thought she was seeing. When she looked back at the bathroom doorway, the woman was still standing there staring at Beth. The woman told Beth, "It will all be all right" before turning and walking into the nearby bathroom. When Beth reached the bathroom doorway and looked in, no one was there. She jumped back into her bed and hid under the covers for the rest of the night.

Beth had never met Edd's mother because she passed away before Edd and Beth married. Edd said he assumed from Beth's description this woman was his mother and his mother's spirit was more than likely there to reassure Beth about their marriage, but he added he was beginning to have doubts about the relationship. This assumption, about his mother's spirit being reassuring to Beth, would soon become a conviction of Edd's. They would both later tell me they had a terrible argument that afternoon and Beth was worried about the marriage. That was the reason she was sleeping alone that particular night.

The email discussed other occurrences in the house. Edd described sounds like "heavy bodies" being dragged across the floor in the family room. This event took place every night for seven nights, always at midnight. Edd wrote when he entered the family room to investigate the noises, the noises would stop and he found nothing. But when he got back into his bed, the sounds would begin again. He wrote the wall behind the family's computer would mumble, making sounds as thought someone was talking but never clear enough to make out what was being said. On Nov. 3, the attention of the pet cats also seemed to be drawn to the mumbling sound coming from the wall. The cat looked at the wall were the sounds originated and then followed it across the dinning area into the living room. While looking in the direction of the sound, the cat's tail puffed out and it began to hiss at seemingly towards the middle of the living room floor, although Edd saw nothing there. The cat raced down the hall into Edd and Beth's bedroom. Beth followed to make sure the cat was all right and as she entered the doorway to her own bedroom, she said the closet door had swung open and nearly hit her in the face.

The email discussed knocking sounds heard in the garage, the master bathroom shower turning on and off by itself, the nearby toilet flushing by itself, toys in the living room, family room and children's bedrooms moving or turning on by themselves. The email also described an unusual cold in the children's bedrooms; TVs that turned themselves off, light bulbs that lasted only a day or two and numerous brown-outs and power surges.

I first suspected these events could be explained away by a simple case of old plumbing and a home needing rewiring. I later wished that had been the case. I decided to do an initial interview and investigation. Then, if we got any readings or anomalous photos, we could see how this family wanted to proceed. If nothing else, we could show this family not all "paranormal phenomenon" is necessarily spirit-related. Our research group knew what to look for and could hopefully be able to ease the family's minds. But there were still the reports of two separate full-body apparitions. I thought over the possibilities. Could they have been related to a dream state, or maybe a reflection of some sort? Or even too much late night horror TV intruding on their subconscious minds? We would find out.

When I phoned Edd the following evening, he said he was glad we decided to come out and have a "look see." He mentioned several other events which had taken place since his initial email. He said he was now convinced the events were connected with his mother. The woman Beth reported seeing standing in the bathroom doorway fit his mother's physical description to a "T," Edd said. Since Edd's mother had passed away from cancer in 1985 before she met Beth or their new daughter, and because he kept no photos of his mother in the house, Edd suspected his mother might somehow be keeping an eye on their infant daughter and making herself known to Beth.

This made some sense to me but I wasn't going to commit to any theories until we had some hard evidence to back up the events. We set a date for the research group to come to the home, and I told Edd to keep a journal of anything suspicious, the email or call me with the details anytime. It was the "anytime" part that would prove to be a great help to the family and result into many intrusions into many nights of sleep.

I first checked the property records for the home. Edd informed me they were renting the house, but Volusia County is very good about making public records accessible. The house was built in 1966 with a 1997 addition, now being used as the family room. It was a typical three-bedroom, two-bath home with a garage. It was concrete block and stucco construction, also standard for Florida. Nothing seemed to be out of the norm until I checked the sales records.

The original owner passed away in the home in 1987. The house was sold to a family member for $100, again not unusual. The house was sold again in 1991 in a qualified sale for $48,000. Not unusual and a fair market price for the year. But that was where the normalcy ended. In 1996, the house was appraised at $49,000, but sold for only $12,700. In 1998, it again sold for $10,600. It was last sold in April 2000 for $14,800. Just two months before, the house next door sold for $87,000. Both houses were similar in size, rooms, number of improvements, and condition. It seemed to me whoever had previously owned this house wasn't too concerned about loosing money on the sale of the home. My thoughts returned to possible bad plumbing and electrical problems. I honestly thought we would pull up to a house needing a great deal of upgrading, repairs and remodeling.

Then another record caught my eye, the permit page. The plumbing had been completely redone in June 1997 and the wiring throughout the house was completed two months later. There went one theory partially out the window. I never completely cross off a theory until I check things out for myself.

I then dug through records of nearby properties, looking for deaths somehow related to the home, nearby homes and surrounding area. Perhaps this seemed a bit silly, but there had to be a reason for the amount of activity this couple reported, if it was in fact of a paranormal origin.

The original owner of the home who had passed away in what was now Edd and Beth's bedroom was an elderly woman who often wore housedresses. The death certificate listed suffocation as the cause of death, but it was not a homicide. This struck me as odd, so I dug deeper. The medical examiners reported she suffocated in her sleep. Apparently, when she turned on her side while sleeping, her face went into a soft pillow and she was unable to breathe. Because she was heavily medicated, it was concluded she was unaware and suffocated. Could she be the woman who was standing in the bathroom doorway staring out at Beth, I thought.

It turns out the nephew of the woman was taking care of his ailing aunt. This same nephew also picked up the house for $100.00 just after his aunt's passing. The nephew also passed away in the house.

He suffered a heart attack at the sink in the master bathroom. In 1991, another relative sold the house to a couple moving to the area from up north. I wasn't sure why this information seemed so important, but I tucked it away for future reference.

Another death close to the home occurred directly across the street. An elderly man who lived in the house had been murdered by his nurse and her boyfriend. This senseless act took place after the man signed a new will naming the nurse as sole beneficiary to his estate. The elderly man visited the woman in the housedresses regularly, neighbors would later recount. Might this man's spirit still be visiting his old friend? Could this be the man Edd saw sitting on his son's bed?

The last death I could locate in the surrounding area was a young construction worker killed in a drunken driving accident on the same street as the Dunnam house. The accident took place two weeks after construction had begun on the family room addition to the house. Since his life ended so quickly and tragically, did his spirit stay on this plane of existence? Could it be possible for the young mans spirit to be attracted to the house because of the familiar work going on there? Was the noise coming from the family room this young man working in the afterlife?

I hoped we could find some answers for this nice young couple who were obviously plagued by something strange in their home. If there is one thing I know about doing paranormal investigations, there are always more questions than answers. I am not one to give up easily and will exhaust every source until I am sure there is no answer to be found. I stay levelheaded and have been the "bubble-burster" on many occasions. I make every effort to assure no man-made source or naturally occurring event can be the cause of supposed paranormal activity. The few times I have drifted off course, group investigators Suzi or Mac always quickly brought me back around.

I also know there is so much in this universe we do not and may never understand. There are also a lot of spirits in this world, more than most people care to admit to or even want to know about. And it seemed the Dunnam house had more than its fair share of them.

The group met at my house at 6:30 p.m. to pack up all the gear we had. At the time, an amount considerably less than eventually acquired throughout the course of this case. During the half-hour drive from Daytona to Deltona, we discussed our plan of action. Ros would take electromagnetic field readings and 35-mm photographs. Suzi would take digital photos as backup to Ros's 35-mm pictures. Macrina would take temperature and humidity readings. Steve would draw a map of the house and grounds while checking for any possible hoaxes. I would get detailed information from the family on their experiences and complete our standard interview questionnaire.

The members of the group discussed the possibility of a hoax and to be sure to take very detailed notes. If a door opened, I wanted to know if there was an open window nearby. If someone felt a cold spot, I wanted to know the exact location of every air conditioning vent in the house. If someone passed gas, I wanted to know when and where it happened. I readily admit I am not an easy person to work with; I pay attention to every detail, whether large or small. Most people never notice the things I easily see. I wanted my researchers sharp, making keen observations, taking tons of notes and keeping each other informed. We always do these things, but for some reason I knew this case was going to be different.

We pulled up in front of the house at 7:15 p.m. Edd came down the walkway to greet us excitedly while he held Emily in his arms. I shook his hand and introduced myself while my fellow researchers began unpacking our equipment from the car. Edd commented on how firm of a handshake I had. I explained to him my father always told me a weak handshake was a sign of weak character, so I have always given a firm handshake. Edd smiled and agreed with my father's handshaking etiquette.

"Must have been a military man, your dad," Edd commented.

"Yes, U.S. Navy," I returned. Edd smiled as he reached for the screen door handle to hold the door open for us.

We all filed through it with our cases full of gadgets and gizmos. Even though we have the latest technology, I still believe in bringing along a sack of flour, candles and string. Technology may fail in certain circumstances, but flour, candles and string won't. Besides, if such things were good enough for the pioneers in this field, why should we discard it just because we have "more advanced" methods?

Beth was in the kitchen finishing up what appeared to be dinner dishes. Edd was greeting the members of the group, loudly apologizing for nearly being late. He had a meeting with a client at Hooters and the men had become a bit distracted. Imagine that, I thought.

Edd is one of those animated tough-guy men. He was fit as a fiddle and ready to rock n roll at a moment's notice; proud to be an American and prouder to have served in the military; the protector of his family, a loving father and husband; hard working and lots of fun to be around.

Beth was the exact opposite of Edd. She was quiet, demure, enjoyed staying at home and taking care of the children and house, and was proud of her husband and family. Edd offered Steve a beer while Beth offered the rest of us soda, chips and dip, and donuts. They were an interesting couple that seemed to be a great match.

I turned down Steve's beer for him explaining we do not drink before, during or after an investigation. I explained to Beth we normally come prepared with coolers full of drinks and snacks, thanking her for her offer. I motioned to the group to get to work and they moved off with their assigned equipment, two-way radios and note pads. I sat in the living room with Edd and Beth having them sign release forms and I began asking the interview questions.

Some of the questions we ask are considered by some to be intrusive, but I feel they are all necessary. Some of our questions are fun and quite like the ones Bill Murray's character asked the librarian in *Ghostbusters*. We often laugh over the librarian's answer, "Well, my uncle thought he was St. Jerome."

I positioned myself in an armchair facing the hallway and its back to a wall against the garage. I had my interview forms, release forms, my journal, pen and a Gauss meter with me. A Gauss meter measures fluctuations in the electromagnetic field, EMF, which many believe indicates spirit activity. There was an end table to my right with a lamp and small fan on it, a few candles, an ashtray, and a candy dish. The couch was adjacent to the chair and ran the length of the wall separating the living room from the kitchen. Beth sat on the end furthest from me. Emily climbed up and down and whined a bit, nothing unusual for an 18-month-old baby. Edd paced between the kitchen and opposite end of the living room. He was smoking a clove cigarette and trying to keep the smoke away from the baby. There was a wing chair up against the far wall and directly opposite the couch was an entertainment center with the TV and VCR, several photos of the children and several Halloween decorations. To my left was a large bin filled with toys for the baby, all those bright colorful noise makers to occupy infant's busy little minds and hands. There were three cats investigating our equipment cases, and a closet just behind the front door. The house was moderately sized and sparsely decorated. It seemed as if they had recently moved into the house, but they had been there since February and this was October.

As I began my standard interview questions I heard a knocking sound on the wall behind me. Edd and Beth barely flinched. I radioed to the group and told them to meet me in the garage. As I went to stand up and head through the kitchen, I picked up my Gauss meter and turned it on. It started clicking away. A "normal" spirit indication generally shows a field reading between 2 and 8 on this instrument. The dial went from a 3 to just above a 6. As I slowly moved it around the area the electromagnetic energy fluctuation lessened to 3.8, then increased to 5.7, dropped again to 4.2, peaked at a 7.4 before stopping altogether.

Steve was the first one to arrive and he watched with me as the needle on the Gauss meter jumped around. He immediately began looking for a source in the living room but found nothing. The lamp produced a 9 and the small fan pegged the needle above 10. I asked Edd what was in the garage directly behind the chair and he replied, "A gas hot water heater." Okay, this had to be the source. If the heater had turned on it may explain the knocking and the jumping around of the reading on the Gauss meter.

16

Steve, Suzi and I headed through the kitchen and into the garage. When I opened the door a cold burst of air hit me. It was 74 degrees outside and there were several windows open in the house. I noted the "breeze" but didn't think of it as a possible paranormal event. The garage was full of furniture: an antique armoire, love seat, desk, and boxes that appeared to contain personal items from a recent move. I yelled into the house, "Edd? Is this all of your stuff out here?"

"Nope, that stuff belongs to the guy that owns this place," he yelled back before joining us.

We made our way to the hot water heater to check it. Edd stood in the doorway chuckling. "That's not what made the knocking sound," he said. The Gauss meter was steady at 1.5. I turned back to Edd. "Oh and how do you know," I asked. "Have you had it checked?"

"Dusty," he explained, "I own a home remodeling company. I do everything from plumbing and electrical to concrete, tile, carpet, roofing, painting. You name it, if it has to do with fixing a house; I'm the man for the job."

Macrina walked into the garage and said, "Has anyone noticed any cold areas yet?"

"Why?" I asked.

"Well, I was just taking readings and the back kids' bedroom had an area where it was 21 degrees Fahrenheit," she said. "As I was writing down the temperature, my EMF went off; got a 3.2. And in the master bedroom I had an area near the bathroom that read 24 degrees and the EMF hit 2.8. I was just wondering if you guys were having anything going on."

"We're checking for a knocking sound, might be the hot water heater, but we're not sure yet," I replied. "Did you check the rest of the house?"

"Yes, I wanted Suzi and Ros to go outside with me and check around the yard to see if we got anything," she said.

"Go for it, Steve and I will hang in here for a while," I replied. "I've got more questions to ask and he needs to finish the map."

During this time Steve checked the water heater for loose wires, loose pipes, anything that might make a knocking sound as the heater turned on. Just then the water heater came on. We all stood back for a moment a watched and listened. I felt kind of stupid standing there, watching a water heater, as if it were going to perform some marvelous feat for us. We watched, waited, the EMF never went above 1.5. We watched and waited, watched and waited and nothing. There was no banging, no rise in the electromagnetic field, nothing.

I gave Steve one of my looks he read to mean 'stick around and check out the garage,' exactly what the look was meant to suggest. Macrina, Suzi and Ros headed outside. I joined Edd, Beth and Emily in the living room. Before I sat back down I turned the Gauss meter back on, just in case.

Edd began to explain the furniture and boxes in the garage. The gentleman who owned the home left his personal belongings behind when he moved out. I must have had a puzzled look on my face because Edd continued in more detail. He said the owner lived in the house for about three months before leaving suddenly at about 3:30 in the morning one day.

"The guy left everything, food in the fridge, toothbrush in its holder, clothes, furniture and everything else he owned here," Edd said. "Just hauled ass out the door in the middle of the night, and refuses to come inside anymore. That should have been our first clue." Beth added when they came to look at the house to rent it, the owner stayed outside in his vehicle. When they signed the lease he asked them to just put his stuff in boxes and leave them in the garage, that he would come by to pick it up. Edd and Beth agreed and whenever he stopped by to pick up the rent he asked for a few boxes. He never came in the house but would just sit out at the curb in his car and wait for either Edd or Beth to bring him the rent and boxes of his belongings.

"Once he came to the front door, but when I opened the door and invited him in, he just shook his head, grabbed the rent check and left," Beth said.

I asked Beth if she ever mentioned any of their experiences to the landlord. "Oh, yes," she said. "When we asked him if he ever heard noises or if there was a reason certain rooms were so cold, he told us this house was not haunted. His exact words were, 'This house is *not* haunted.' We never said anything about it being haunted. It just struck me funny when he popped out with such a quick and precise answer. Edd asked him if there was anything here that might be a danger to the children, and he repeated, 'This house is not haunted.' Then he left."

I could see this discussion upset Beth. She held Emily tighter to her and toyed with her hair nervously, so I went back to my interview questions. As I got to the final question, "What do you believe is going on in the house," the EMF jumped to 5.3 and knocking started on the wall again. I jumped up out of the chair and began to look for a mouse, rat, or kid's toy, anything that could make the knocking sound. Nothing. I radioed Steve.

"Steve, you still in the garage," I asked.

"Yes," he replied.

"Did you hear that?"

"Hear what?"

"The knocking on the wall?"

"No. There's no noise out here and I'm standing right next to the water heater."

"Can you get in here and listen to this?"

"On my way."

Steve was in the living room in 3 seconds flat. He stood there for a moment looking at the wall, trying to determine the source of the noise. He stepped past me and moved the chair, checked on and under the end table, moved the bin of toys, and finally backed up looking puzzled. The Gauss meter was still clicking away between 3.2 and 5.8. I reached out to touch the wall at where I believed the center of the knocking to be coming from and suddenly it stopped.

"Okay, well, I'm not sitting over there anymore," I said.

Edd laughed, "You'll get used to it, Dusty."

I asked Steve to set up an audio recorder in the boys' bedroom to see if we might catch an electronic voice phenomenon, an EVP. We have three different pieces of equipment for trying to catch "spirit voices" on tape. One is a simple handheld tape recorder which uses standard audio tapes. The second one is a larger recorder that also uses regular audio tapes but with a microphone on a 16-foot cord. And the third is a digital voice recorder which uses a Smart Media card to store the recordings. After the completion of this case, we purchased a Sony omni-directional microphone that picks up sounds from all directions instead of just from straight ahead like our standard microphone.

Steve headed off to the back of the house with the large recorder and a new audio tape. I set up the small handheld recorder in the living room next to the wall where the knocking sounds where coming from.

Edd said the sounds that occurred in the middle of the night seem to come from the family room. I grabbed my journal, pen and Gauss meter and followed him towards the family room. As he began to lead me out to the family room, I paused for a moment at the breakfast bar to take a good long chug of my soda, when I felt something pull my hair. This wasn't just one or two hairs being gently pulled, it was a handful of hair being yanked, yanked hard enough for my head to jerk back. This would become a very familiar event at the Dunnam house. I quickly turned around, the Gauss meter in my pocket ticking away at what I assumed was a 2 by the sound of the clicking noise coming from my pocket, but there was no one there. Surprise, surprise!

I said, "Okay, who ever just pulled my hair, I acknowledge you are here, there is no need to yank on my hair so hard." I had the feeling I was being watched; it was eerie. The EMF stopped clicking, so I kept my composure and set my soda can down to follow Edd into the family room.

I stepped through the sliding glass door and instantly noticed the cold. This room was freezing! I radioed Macrina and asked her if she had taken a temperature reading of the room. She replied, "Yes, it was 76 degrees." Seventy-six degrees my aunt fanny, I thought. This room couldn't be more than 40 right now. I radioed Steve and asked when he was done setting up the tape recorder please bring the other temperature gauge into the family room. He was on his way back down the hall when I radioed and he joined us in the family room within seconds. He reset the gauge and we watched the temperature reading drop to 43 degrees.

The family room was a simple addition to the house. Most of us in the "Sunshine State" call these rooms "Florida rooms." They normally have a sliding glass door from the main house and another door to the outside back yard or patio. They often have windows all around for optimal bird or weather watching and aren't generally well insulated. With no insulation, it was 74 degrees outside, why was this room so cold, I thought. There were no air conditioning vents, no ceiling fans, just a small oscillating fan in the far corner of the room near a mattress on the floor. Edd's oldest son had taken this room as his own personal space. To the right of the sliding glass door was a shelf with clothes and books and to the left, a desk. At the end of the desk was the door to the outside and on the far side of it was a dresser with a TV and Nintendo system. There was a small night table next to the mattress and some clothes strewn about the floor, a typical teenage boy's room. There were closed vertical blinds on all the windows. Steve looked behind each blind to see if the windows were open or broken. They were all closed and intact.

It began to feel warmer in the room and I looked back over at the temperature gauge. It now read 59 degrees.

Edd said laughingly, "Well, whoever was just here must have left." Just then the blinds at the center of the largest section of window moved. Not just a little, they moved like the window was open and a strong gust of wind had just blown through. They jumped around and moved away from the windowsill approximately three inches, making a terribly loud rattling sound. Steve checked the window again and confirmed it was closed tight and assured there was no air coming from elsewhere in the room.

Just then we heard Suzi's voice over the radio, "Um, I think you guys might want to get out here."

"Where are you?" I replied.

"The backyard."

"We're on our way."

21

As I walked along the garage side of the house I could see the cameras flashing almost continuously. The gate leading to the back yard was open and we walked through it to find Ros, Suzi and Macrina snapping pictures and taking temperature readings like lunatics.

"What's going on?" I asked.

"Watch this," Suzi said as she held the camera out in front of her and snapped a picture of the back of the house. We never look through the viewfinder, a habit I picked up early on. That way you can watch for sparkles in the flash. When the flash went off you could see hundreds of sparkles of light in instant. In Florida, paranormal researchers need to be careful of high humidity producing this same effect. But this was October and the humidity was very low, only 38 percent. It is thought in the paranormal field these sparkles indicate spirit activity. The only way you will know for sure is when photograph film is developed. That is, unless you're also using a digital camera as back up. Then you could look in the LCD screen and immediately see if you have results. And we were. We viewed the photos Suzi took with the digital camera and sure enough, there was a thick mist over the family room and orbs all over the backyard. This still wasn't proof though. We'd have to wait to see the 35-mm shots.

Macrina said, "If you think that's something, have a look at this." She had two temperature gauges with her. She had placed a small unit on top of a canoe sitting about 12 feet from the outside wall of the family room while she held a laser-sighted thermal scanner. The unit on the canoe showed 73 degrees. The thermal scanner picked up three separate locations on the house reading between 32.8 degrees and 54.3 degrees. This made no sense to me. Why would the house be so much colder than the air temperature? They didn't have the AC on because it was a beautiful night. A few windows were open in the front of the house, and several small fans were on, but this was a major temperature fluctuation as far as we could tell.

It was now nearly 10 p.m. We finished jotting our notes, collecting equipment and started packing our bags. I sat in the living room with Edd and Beth for a few minutes and assured them I would return. I told them I would call them in a day or so to let them know if we had gotten anything on the audio tape, 35-mm film or digital photos. I also reminded them if they needed to call me, day or night for any reason, to feel free to do so. I urged them to keep a journal or log of events for me. I also said I wished we could stay longer this night, but we all had day jobs early in the morning. Next time we would stay longer, possibly all night. They were both happy at the prospect of someone else being in the house overnight, someone else to witness these strange events that occurred throughout the night. I flipped through my day planner and set our next date for further investigating at Nov. 7. They seemed somewhat relieved, and obviously still frightened. Beth hugged me and said, "Thank you, I feel a little better about all this."

Edd also hugged me and said, "Dusty, I am so glad you came here tonight. I was really starting to think I was loosing it. I just want to know that I'm not going crazy, well, crazier than I already am." He laughed and walked with me out to my car. Beth and Emily waved good-bye from the inside of the closed screen door.

As we drove away I felt a deep empathy for this family. There did seem to be something going on, but what it was, I wasn't sure of, yet. The group remained quiet for about half the drive home. I finally broke the silence with a question. "So, what do you guys think is going on at that house?" There was silence for a few minutes, and then Ros spoke up.

"Well dude, I'm not saying it's ghosts, yet, but there is something weird going on there," she said in her casual style. "Those cold spots were so weird. And that mist over the back of the house, incredible!"

Suzi joined in, "Yeah, that mist was too much. It moved around with the temperature drops, it was very cool. What do you guys think that was all about?"

"Screw the mist, that friggin' knocking got to me. I couldn't figure out where it was coming from or what it was," Steve said.

"That unnerved me a bit too, but my hair getting pulled was too much, I almost lost it right then," I said.

Macrina, Suzi and Ros talked in the backseat while Steve and I discussed how to proceed with the case in the front seat. I was anxious to get home to look at the digital photos and listen to the audio recording to see if we had gotten any results. There was the film to drop off at Walgreen's One-hour photo the following morning. I had a routine I went through at the One-hour photo counter. I would ask them to print the photos even if they were dark, and not to cut the negatives. Early on, I got some strange looks but now they knew me by name and no longer thought I was insane. They even saved anomalous photos from other customers to show me. I have come to appreciate the photo technicians Nick, Susan and Donna's patience and extra care with my photos and me.

As I pulled up in front of my house, I sat for a moment and thought about the events of the evening. Maybe it was instinct, maybe intuition, but I knew somewhere down deep inside, this case was going to become very interesting very fast.

Chapter Two:
Initial Documentation

After I got the equipment put away, said "Hi" to my dog, checked phone messages and got a cold drink, I headed straight to my computer with digital camera in hand. I sat while my old steam engine style computer warmed up. It doesn't really run off of a steam engine, but its close. It was built in 1984, has a 500-megabyte hard drive that has been upgraded to a whopping two-gigabyte hard drive and a 13-inch monitor. But, she works just fine for me. I use a photo-editing program called *ACDSee* for all my photos. Now when I say, photo editing I don't mean I alter our photos, I do not. The only adjustment I make is to resize them, lighten them a bit if they are too dark and to drop in our copyright. I keep one copy of the original photo and one edited copy so no one can say I've changed the photos to add in orbs, mists or anything else.

I had no expectations as I began to view the photos from the Dunnam house. We had taken two rolls of 35-mm film and 53 digital photos. The number variation is due to the flash not going off on the digital camera. If it doesn't go off, another photo of the same location is taken. The first couple of photos were unremarkable but when I viewed the fourth photo there was a bright orb inside the closet in Edd and Beth's room: the same closet door that opened and nearly hit Beth in the face.

This was good, but nothing to write home about. I checked over everyone's notes to see if they had gotten any readings when this photo was taken, and sure enough, the EMF read 3.1 and the temperature was 14 degrees lower in this room at the time. We generally take temperature readings every 15 minutes or so depending on what else may be going on. When Macrina first took the temperature in this room it was 76 degrees. When this photo was taken it was 62 degrees and shortly after it was back up to 74 degrees. I noted there were no open windows in this room, the ceiling fan wasn't on and the small fan on the night table was not turned on.

The next digital photo of interest was taken during the first round of knocking in the living room and fluctuating Gauss meter. This photo showed two orbs over the couch where Beth and Emily had been sitting, one of them moving. I didn't see this photo as real evidence since the knocking event occurred about six feet to the right of the orbs in the photo.

My mouth dropped open when I saw the first photo taken in the backyard. It showed a huge mist with several very bright light emitting orbs. One appeared to be about the size of a basketball and moving towards the garage area. While Steve was still in the garage and I was hearing the second round of knocking on the wall in the living room, Suzi had snapped this digital photo on her way into the backyard.

The next photo was taken of the same location. It showed nothing of interest, no mist, no orbs, just the corner of the house and the gate. The next one taken from behind the garage showed two very bright orbs directly over the roof of the garage.

As I continued through the photos and flipping through everyone's notes, I soon realized we were going to need more camera equipment. We had never worked a case with paranormal activity occurring simultaneously in different locations. If this were going to be the norm at the Dunnam house, I would need to be better prepared for our next visit.

At this time we were using a Hewlett-Packard *315* digital camera and a Pentax *IQ Zoom* 35-mm camera. Shopping for new equipment has never been an issue for me. Coming up with the cash is another story. Most of our equipment is moderately priced, but some is very expensive. Since we never charge a fee for doing investigations, we rely on donations and my spare change to purchase new equipment.

The next interesting photo I came to was taken outside of the family room. This was the thickest mist I had ever seen, either personally or in a photograph. The notes indicated this was when Edd, Steve and I were in the family room sensing the cold and the vertical blind movement. This photo is why I was called outside. After seeing the photo, I saw I was called with good reason. I sat and stared at the photo for several minutes on my small computer monitor not really believing what my eyes were seeing. Could whatever was causing the strange occurrences in the Dunnam home be a part of this heavy mist we had photographed? Could this rather large display be from one elderly lady or one elderly man? Even if we narrowed it down to the construction worker who passed away nearby, this mist was almost overwhelming. I knew we had stumbled onto something more than a residual haunting.

The next photo was taken while we documented the strange cold spots on the back of the house. I wasn't sure at the time what this rainbow was doing over the peak of the Dunnam house roof, but I would later come to find out. If you were to draw a line through the rainbow down through the roof into the house, this spot would be at the bookcase in the hallway. This too would later become an important fact.

The final digital photo from our first night at the Dunnam home showed Steve in the small back bedroom. This is the same bedroom where Edd reportedly saw a man sitting on the end of his son's bed. This photo was taken as Steve went back into the room to retrieve the tape recorder. Ros happened to be standing in the hallway when she heard his EMF start clicking and snapped the photo. The photo showed Steve holding the Gauss meter above his head and a large bright orb right next to it. The orb was moving fast across the room towards the outside wall of the house. Steve and Ros's notes reflected EMF reading to be 2.8. They also noted the ceiling fan and light were turned off by a switch on the wall. Ros further noted the temperature in the room was only 68 degrees but the hallway where she was standing was reading 75 degrees.

After seeing what we had documented, I couldn't wait for morning to take the 35-mm film to Walgreen's. Since I had eight hours to wait, I decided to listen to the tape recording to see if we had gotten any EVP. I readied the tape recorder and headphones and grabbed my note pad and pen. I sat on the edge of the bed and turned the volume all the way up. I listened to Steve report the location, time, date and placement of the recorder. He listed the people in the house and said he would be closing the door behind him. I heard him set the recorder down and close the bedroom door. I kept hearing a "click" sound, but couldn't make out what might be causing it. I knew the ceiling fan hadn't been turned on, so it couldn't be the cord hitting the light globe. I knew the windows were not open, so it couldn't be the vertical blinds moving due to a breeze. I pictured the room in my mind and couldn't grasp what could be causing this irregular click sound. I counted each time I heard the click on the tape. The sound was present 13 times on the 90-minute tape. I made a note in my journal to go over the room on our next visit with a fine-toothed comb to see if I could determine the source of the noise.

I finally went to bed around 3:00 a.m., setting my alarm to get up at nine o'clock to drop off the film. I tossed and turned all night, my thoughts kept going back to the sounds in the house. The knocking and the clicking we caught on tape. I walked over every inch of both rooms in my mind and still couldn't make sense of the noises. I don't like unanswered questions and these noises plagued me for at least another week. There were also the cold spots, mist, orbs, the hair pulling, the moving vertical blinds, and a frightened young couple with a small child. Was this house truly haunted and if so, why? It made no sense one person's spirit could be in different locations causing simultaneous paranormal events. I have come to learn there are no set rules or guidelines to follow where spirit activity is concerned. Spirits will do what they want, when they want and how they want. If you're not ready and patient, you will miss them.

I woke up feeling not well rested. I turned on the coffeepot, let the dog out, hit the bathroom before heading out for Walgreen's. There was a line at the photo counter and I waited impatiently. I tried to keep my mind focused on the Dunnam house, but a woman at the head of the line was causing a commotion. She was picking up film from the overnight service and also had what looked like her weekly groceries. She argued with the teller about a 10-cent discrepancy over some obscure item I could care less about. Finally I had enough so I opened my purse, reached into my wallet, grabbed a dime and walked up and slammed it onto the counter. "Listen, there are more people here waiting," I said. "It's worth the dime to get you out of this line." The other customers in line actually applauded. The woman cursed and called me a "bitch," like that's never happened to me before. She grabbed her bags and left.

When my turn arrived, I stated my usual request to, "Print them even if they're dark and don't cut the negatives." The clerk informed me they were backed up and I could pick the photos up at noon. Noon, I thought. This set my already foul mood into overdrive, but I kept my cool and left.

I returned home to make a badly-needed cup of coffee and sat at my computer to check my email. I deleted eight emails wanting me to work from home on my computer. Another three emails referring to some celebrity's naked photos and six emails containing other obscure advertisements were zapped. I noticed among all the useless email filling my mailbox, I had one email from Edd. He thanked the group for coming out to have a look at their home. He wrote they heard the knocking only one more time before they went to bed. And at 3:00 a.m. they heard the "heavy bodies being dragged across the floor" of the family room again. Otherwise, it was a quiet night.

Quiet? Okay, if that was their definition of quiet, who was I to say different? I noted Edd's writing style. His punctuation consisted of only periods at the end of sentences. He had bad grammar, used no capitalization and obviously didn't use spell check. So far, every email Edd sent was addressed to "Dusty," and signed "Edd." I replied to his email, thanking him for inviting us. I reminded him they could call anytime and we would return on Nov. 7 at about 8:30 p.m. prepared to stay the entire night.

I finished my second cup of coffee, took a shower and got dressed. It was just after noon when I headed back up to Walgreen's. I walked through the door and noticed the store was packed; it must have been the first day of a great money saving sale. The old saying of "a watched pot never boils" holds true for pictures, too. Anxiously-awaited photos never seem to develop. I learned that after I'd dropped the film off, there had been some technical difficulty with the processing machine and there would be an extra 20-minute wait. I roamed the aisles of the store, trying not to be anxious. When I returned to the photo counter, the pictures were finally ready.

I returned home and carefully opened the package. As I flipped through the prints I saw no positive results at first. This isn't unusual since digital cameras often capture more than what is visible or even spirit activity. Digital cameras also capture dust and high levels of humidity. This is why we don't rely on digital photos as sole evidence. Out of the 48 photos we had taken three showed positive results. Two were too dark to use as evidence, but one was clear and useable. As Suzi, Ros and Macrina ventured outside to the back yard, one of them managed to catch a bright, beautiful orb directly over the garage area. I checked back through their notes and found this was when Steve and I were still checking on the knocking sound in the garage.

This was still not solid evidence of a haunting but our corresponding data was starting to look relatively good. We had EMF levels in the "right" range, unexplainable audible sounds, measurable cold spots, 35-mm and digital photos showing activity and it all connected together with a paranormal event we had witnessed. I was now beginning to look forward to our next trip to the Dunnam house.

I began making preparations for our next visit. I purchased another 35-mm camera, two more EMF detectors, another temperature gauge, another digital voice recorder, and a Fuji *FinePix 2300* digital camera. I bought tons of blank audio tapes, batteries and film. I even was able to secure an 8mm camcorder from a pawnshop along with accessories for only $100. I also purchased two *X-10* night-vision surveillance cameras, two VCR's to record them and a small used TV to use as a viewing monitor. I contacted all the group members to see who was available to spend an entire night at the house. I told them of the results in case anyone was not comfortable with the activity. It is imperative all of my researchers stay in a positive frame of mind and keep alert. If they didn't feel up to it, I wanted to know now. Macrina, Ros, Suzi and Steve said they were ready for the challenges we might face on our first overnight in the Dunnam house. We were ready to spend the night.

Chapter Three:
First Overnight Experience

The morning dawned bright as the sun came through my bedroom window, I could hear the birds singing…Wait, wrong story. I am and have always been a night person. I don't really start waking up until 10 p.m. With the need to hold down a daytime job and keep my nights free for research and investigations, I tend to get to bed at a pretty decent hour. I normally try to stay up as late as I can for a day or so before we do an overnighter to prepare me for a night of no sleep. I normally stay up until 2 a.m., but on nights I do an investigation, I may stay up until 5 a.m. or 6 a.m. My usual schedule is to get up at 9 or 10 o'clock in the morning, but not on nights prior to cases. I sleep as late as I can so my body is more used to staying up all night for the case.

Contrary to popular belief, you cannot make a living as a paranormal investigator. You need to hold down some mundane job to pay your bills unless you're a PhD who works for a foundation or university. I work Monday through Thursday from 10 to 6 for a small local herb company. It's mostly boring, always repetitive, work but it keeps the bills paid so I can do the job I truly enjoy. After the sun goes down, I begin the job I hold such a deep passion for: paranormal research.

I began my normal pre-overnight routine around 4 p.m. I went over every piece of equipment to assure they were in proper working order. I changed every battery so we would start out the night with fully charged batteries. I made sure we had plenty of fresh film, audio and video tapes. I printed out enough investigation logs and maps of the Dunnam house so each member had their own copy. I packed the flashlights, candles and anything else I thought we might need for the upcoming night. I packed my journal book, favorite pen and cooler full of diet Mountain Dew. I was sure to grab a spare pack of cigarettes and plenty of munchies for the long night ahead. I checked the moon phase and found it was waning in Leo and one day short of going into third quarter. There were M-class solar flares and the geomagnetic levels were active. I always check these phases and levels since there may be some sort of pattern associated with them that aide other paranormal researchers. I placed stones and pennies in my pocket, a habit I picked up early on. This habit is said to protect the carrier from harm negative or angry spirits might try to inflict. Maybe it sounds a bit silly or superstitious to carry these items on a scientific investigation, but I believe it works. And the power of the mind can work miracles when fear is involved.

The group members arrived on time and helped me to load the equipment into the trunk of my car. I didn't have as many hands as I hoped, Macrina and Suzi had been called into work unexpectedly, but the three of us would be just fine. I grabbed my purse and pillow on my way out the door and told my dog to behave. We packed the rest of our essentials and our bodies into the car and headed towards the setting sun. We reviewed our plans as I drove the 23 miles to Deltona. I made my usual speech about keeping the location and documentation secure from long hair, camera straps, smoke and the rest of the intrusive things which can corrupt data. Even though I smoke and do so heavily, I never smoke where photos are taken or video is recorded. If the homeowner doesn't smoke, I won't ask to smoke inside their home. I may smoke a lot, but the research is more important to me than getting a nicotine fix. I couldn't say how Edd and Beth would react since they both smoked, but I would give them a gentle reminder not to smoke around the photographic or video equipment. It would make any evidence we get useless to us.

When we pulled up at the house, Beth and Emily were standing inside the front screen door. I waved as we got out of the car and walked around the car to the trunk. Once inside with all of our gear, I sat for several minutes with Beth to talk about new happenings in the home. She said the cat heard a noise in the wall behind the computer and followed it into the living room. She also mentioned the heavy dragging noise that seemed to come from the family room. She said it had worsened since our last visit and now happened nightly. This was great, I thought to myself. Hopefully, we would be on the location when the noise took place.

Beth flipped through some notes and added, "Oh, yeah. On November First, Edd and I heard a woman talking in our bedroom. It was pretty loud, but we still couldn't make out exactly what she was saying, if that makes any sense." I nodded and told her to continue.

"Anyhow, Emily was playing with her toys on the living room floor and she heard it too," Beth continued. "She got up and walked down the hall towards our bedroom. Edd and I got up quickly and followed her down the hallway but we lost sight of her when she went into our room. Edd turned into the room next and he said Emily went into our bathroom. Just then I walked into the room and the closet door swung open fast. It hit me on the right arm and scared me to death."

"Oh my God, are you all right," I asked, knowing Beth was pregnant.

"Yeah, it just scared me," she replied. "I didn't get cut or bruised, just scared. Afterwards, Edd turned around to see if I was okay and I noticed Emily coming out of our bathroom. She had a look on her face like something just scared her. She was pouting and starting to cry. Edd picked her up, but it didn't seem to help. He talked to her to try to calm her down and bounced her; you know, up and down. She just kept whining and pointing into our bathroom.

"He took her out of our bedroom and I looked around in our bathroom for a few minutes, checking to make sure the window was locked and no one was behind the shower curtain. I didn't see anything unusual or anything, but just then the shower turned on. It was weird, too weird for me. I went back out into the living room and told Edd to go fix the shower. He just looked at me like I was crazy and went back to our bathroom to see what the heck I was talking about. He came back less than a minute later and told me the shower wasn't on and it wasn't even dripping or wet. Is that normal?"

"Nothing is really ever normal when you are dealing with paranormal experiences," I said. "It is rare and unusual to have something of that nature occur. About how long did the shower stay on?"

"I really don't know, a few seconds, maybe," she replied. "I didn't stay in there with a stopwatch or anything. It really scared me when it came on, so I just left the room as fast as I could."

"Has this ever happened before?" I inquired further.

"Just once," she said, "when we first moved in, but that time, it didn't scare me, I thought one of the boys left it on, or possibly even Edd. I don't know if Edd ever mentioned it to you or not, but some nights our bedroom TV will turn on by itself too usually when we're, ya know, having sex."

"Why didn't you call me?" I asked. "I'm not that far away, and even if I couldn't come right over, at least I'm a good shoulder to lean on, especially when you're scared."

"I thought about it, but I just didn't want to bother you," she answered.

"Bother me? Bother me? Please, Beth, bother me," I replied. "This is part of the job. If you're scared and need or want to talk, pick up the phone. Please, promise me that if anything even remotely like this happens again you'll call me, no matter what time of day or night it is."

"Okay, we will," she said as she picked up Emily, hugging her again.

Just then, Edd opened the front door with a bang and a smile. "Emme! Sweet Mama! Dusty! Hey gang," he shouted. "Did Beth tell you what happened in the last week? Man this shit is freaky! I swear I'm going nuts! I feel like a 12-year-old girl that's afraid to go to sleep at night."

Edd leaned over and kissed Beth on the cheek before grabbing Emily and tossing her into the air. Emily giggled with delight.

"Sorry I'm late," he said. "I had to run the boys back to their mom's house and I hit some wicked traffic on the way back. They're a kind of freaked by all of this, so I figured it would be best if they weren't here when you guys arrived."

"How ya holding up Edd?" I asked.

"Lemme tell ya Dusty, this shit is freaking me out," he responded seriously. "Being a Ranger and a bouncer in some pretty rough bars for several years never prepared me for this stuff. I really thought I could handle anything, but man, this shit is just, phew, way out there."

Edd told of the mumbling noise in the wall which moved out to the living room then down the hall into their bedroom. As he talked, he showed the path he and the cat made.

Edd is a very animated person who rarely leaves out details. I attributed this to his days as a bouncer. Most bar bouncers learn to watch for subtle things: details about bar patrons, the moves they make to anticipate an action an unruly patrons may take. Edd's training as an Army Ranger taught him to expect and plan for the unexpected. Edd explained he'd checked all the wiring associated with the computer, made sure the desk wasn't somehow bumping against the wall, checked in the bathroom to make sure nothing was out of sorts. He had also checked the family room to make sure one of the boys hadn't left the TV or a radio on. His arms swung in large gestures to demonstrate the path the sound made from the wall to the living room and finally down the hallway into the master bedroom. I learned early on when someone explains these experiences, they add several emotions; fear and disbelief among the two most prominent. Although I believed the family had experienced something that night, I couldn't allow their emotions to rule over what had occurred. Nor could I allow their emotions to sway my perception of the event Edd was now so animatedly describing.

I found over the weeks and months we worked on this case, it was good to hear the descriptions of the events from both Edd and Beth. Not just to get their personal take on what occurred, but because Edd was so animated and Beth was so laid back, it was like having a gauge to find the middle ground between both of them. Edd's exaggerations were countered by Beth's reserve. It was a working balance for some time with this case. Edd would also notice some details Beth missed or had forgotten or vice versa. My greatest challenge with witnesses was Emily. She had for some reason, begun to refuse to speak. It started just before Edd had initially emailed me. She still made her food, toy, diaper and bottle needs known, but had stopped speaking "baby-ese" with the family members. She did however hold conversations and play with unseen guests of the Dunnam house.

We took our usual initial readings throughout the house and yard, but nothing seemed unusual. There were no EMF peaks, no temperature fluctuations, nothing out of the ordinary. I checked the boys' back bedroom for anything that could have possibly made the clicking sound and discovered nothing. I did notice one odd thing. There was no echo in Emily's bedroom; it was like dead air. We noted the readings and set up video and audio equipment. We placed the 8-mm video camera in the living room focused down the hallway. We aimed an *X-10* night vision camera in the family room to focus from the furthest corner past the sliding glass doors into the dining and living room area. I like to overlap my video shots in case we catch something moving on one, we might be lucky enough to pick it up as it moves from one field of view to another. We also set up the tape recorder with the freestanding microphone in the family room. Steve set up the digital voice recorder on the bookshelf in the hallway. Ros was to spend the night in the back bedroom where Edd had seen the male figure sitting on the bed. She would be armed with an EMF, 35-mm camera and a tape recorder. Steve and I would man the living room, dining room, kitchen, garage, hallway and front bathroom. We would turn tapes over, check on noises and take regular temperature and EMF readings in those rooms. Steve had the laser sighted thermal scanner and an EMF. I had a 35-mm camera, digital camera and another EMF.

As I finished my second round I passed by the kitchen and noticed a small toy on the breakfast bar. This snapped my memory into gear and I asked Beth if any of Emily's toys made a clicking sound.

"Yes, that one in front of you makes a clicking sound when it rolls," she answered.

"Does this thing use batteries?" I asked.

"Nope, it just rolls on its own," she explained. "When it rolls, the wheels click and the wings light up. This seems to be their favorite toy. Just about every morning I find it in the middle of the family room floor or in the hallway. At first I thought I had just forgotten to put it away, but then I realized I did put it away with the rest of Emily's toys the night before."

"Do you remember it being in the boys' back bedroom at anytime recently?"

"Yeah, now that you mention it," she replied. "The morning after your last visit I found it in the middle of Alex's bedroom floor. I thought it was odd, because Emily doesn't go in there and the boys hadn't been here."

"Mind if I try an experiment with it?" I asked.

"Not at all, if it helps find out what's going on in our home, I'm all for it," she replied.

I slowly wheeled the toy, a colorful bee-shaped thing, across the breakfast bar. I wanted to hear and see just what this toy would do at a slow speed. The clicks it made did sound similar to those I'd heard on the tapes from our previous visit, but I wasn't sure they were made by this toy. I headed over to the equipment cases and grabbed two black plastic lawn and leaf bags and the bag of flour. I began to spread the lawn and leaf bags out as evenly as I could in the middle of the family room floor. When done, I stepped back a bit to admire the job I had done and noticed everyone standing in the doorway looking at me like I just arrived from Mars. I explained I was going to sprinkle flour onto the bags and leave the toy in the middle to see if anyone unseen played with the toy overnight. And because I didn't want to just throw flour all over Beth's carpet, the bags would protect it.

Steve and Ros had a look of approval on their faces as they turned away to return to the living room. Beth had her hand on her chest like I might ruin her carpet, but I quickly assured her if I did get any flour on the carpet, I would clean it up in the morning.

Edd said, "Damn Dusty! That's cool! Wonder if whoever or whatever it is will play with Emily's toy tonight?"

As I finished putting the final touches on my flour and trash bag artwork, Steve loudly called to me to come into the living room. I walked the few steps into the area and saw everyone looking at the wall. I heard it. The knocking was back. Steve's EMF was reading between 2.8 and 4.2. I took the EMF and asked him to go check the garage again. He took the thermal scanner and left the room. I stepped closer to the wall and the EMF jumped to 5.3. As I stepped a little closer it went down to 2.2. The knocking continued when Steve radioed nothing out of the ordinary happening in the garage, except for the cold. It was 72 degrees outside and the garage was reading 48. Steve said he could see his breath as he exhaled. Four minutes later, he reported the room had warmed to 69 degrees. The EMF showed no further reading and the knocking sound stopped. It was just before 9 p.m.

We went outside to take readings and photos. The temperature dropped slightly to 70 degrees outside, nice weather, but long-time residents needed a sweater or light jacket. Steve scanned with the thermal scanner and found the cold spots from our first trip were no longer present. There was a cold spot on the back corner of the garage, showing 24 degrees. Ros carefully screened the area with an EMF. It spiked to 4.7 at the back of the family room, so I snapped a few photos. I looked at the LCD screen on the back of the digital and there was what appeared to be our rainbow again.

The bright spot to the left and down a bit from the blue rainbow in the above photo is a bug of some sort. This is an all too common anomaly, especially if Florida. I get hundreds of photos sent to me every month from people who think they have caught something strange and unusual on film or digital, only to have it turn out to be a bug.

When Ros moved over by the birdfeeder, the EMF gave a mere 2.8. I snapped photos. As we took our readings, the man who lived to the left of Edd and Beth came out of his back door and looked towards us. I assumed to try to figure out what the heck we were doing taking photos in the dark in Edd and Beth's backyard. Edd walked over quickly to explain we were visiting relatives who had just arrived into town. His neighbor asked why we were taking pictures of what seemed to be nothing but a few bushes and a birdfeeder at such a late hour. I couldn't hear the remainder of the conversation, just bits and pieces of it although the word "nuts" came up. I saw Edd's neighbor go back into his house as Edd turned and started walking back towards me.

"What did you tell him Edd?" I asked.

He laughed. "At first I thought I should just tell him that you guys were visiting. But then I couldn't help myself, I told him there was some weird shit going on in the house late at night, and you guys were here to check into what was causing it."

"And do I dare ask what his response was?"

"He's cool, just an old guy," Edd said. "He mentioned people move in and out over here pretty fast. He told me not to think he was nuts, but he always thought this place was haunted. I told him after the shit I've seen over the past few months, it wouldn't surprise me if you guys did find out the place was in fact haunted."

"I see," I replied. "Well, it's up to you what you tell your neighbors Edd, you're the one who has to live here, not me."

"I kinda wanna tell everyone," he said, "just to make it more real somehow, but at the same time I don't want anyone to know 'cause they'll think I'm nuts"

Edd put his hands in his pockets and began staring at the back of the house. Steve handed Edd the thermal scanner and showed him how to use it, I assumed to get Edd's mind off of whatever he was dwelling on. I told him we hadn't gotten any digital photos of the heavy mist this time and he snapped to attention. He pointed the thermal scanner at the peak of the roof and started talking to the house. "Hey, if you guys are here, we wanna see you. Dusty's trying to take some pictures of you. What's the problem? You're gonna be a no show tonight?" As Ros walked past Edd and Beth, her EMF registered a 4.8. I snapped a 35-mm picture then a digital. There were orbs all around Edd and Beth on the camera's LCD screen.

We always talk to the house or whatever is dwelling in the house, but this was so odd, like whomever or whatever was there actually listened to Edd. The thermal scanner showed no temperature variation, the EMF went silent so we walked back into the house. When we all got in and shut the front door Beth remarked, "Edd, did you turn the TV off when we went outside?"

"Nope, must have been the ghosties again," he laughed, reaching for the remote to turn the TV back on.

"Again?" Ros asked.

"Yeah the TV turns off by itself sometimes," Beth explained. "Edd's checked the outlet and switches even the breakers, we've had the cable company out five times, we have even bought a brand new TV and VCR, but sometimes it just shuts off. The one in our bedroom turns on by itself sometimes."

Ros picked up the remote. As she did, the knocking started again and her EMF went off, just a few seconds this time. Steve didn't even get into the garage by the time the knocking sound ended. I took more pictures in the hopes something might turn up. Sure enough, there was an orb just to the left of where the knocking sound seemed to originate. Steve found nothing in the garage and the EMF lay silent. I decided it was time to settle in and hit the record buttons on the video and audio equipment.

It was just past 10 p.m. when Ros told me she was going to take a smoke break at the breakfast bar. Steve was in the kitchen getting ice for his soda. Edd and Beth were winding down, watching TV in the living room and I was just wandering around the house hitting the record buttons on audio and video equipment. As I came out of the hallway into the living room I saw Ros jump. "Oh my God dude, did you see that?" she said, pointing down to her knee. I looked and saw a bright small light, but only for an instant.

"What did you see Ros?" I asked.

"There was like this little ball of light just circling around me right about this level," she answered, using her hand to show the level around her knees and the movement it made. "I don't know what it was dude, but it was freaky."

"The video is running and at a great angle to catch it," I said. "When we have a look at the tapes, maybe your little light friend will be on the tape."

"Yeah, maybe," she said.

For the first time Ros seemed to have a bit of fear in her. Not that she would let anyone know, but I knew. I have been friends with Ros for several years and knew her moods pretty well. I walked back into the living room and watched as she looked down towards her knees. She finished her cigarette and began to gather equipment and personal items she needed for her night in the back bedroom. She went into the front bathroom to wash her face and brush her teeth. When she came out she had a funny look on her face. I took her aside to ask if she was all right.

"I'm fine," she said. "I just felt like I was being watched while I was in the bathroom. I'm okay dude. Really, I'm keeping it together."

"Okay, but if anything happens or you don't feel comfortable in that room at anytime, radio or get your ass back out here tonight, okay?" I replied.

"No worries, I'll be fine. Night everybody." With that, Ros headed down the hall.

Edd stood up from his easy chair. "Well kiddies, I'm off too. Six O'clock comes early. You guys need anything before I hit it?"

"Nope, we're fine Edd," I said. "Try to get some sleep."

"Shit! With you on guard all night, this will be the first night I will feel okay about falling asleep in this house," he said as he kissed Beth good night then headed down the hallway.

Beth watched TV silently while Steve and I put fresh batteries in the handheld equipment. Beth said, "Do you think we are crazy? Are we loosing our minds?" I sat down in Edd's easy chair.

"Nope, you're not crazy and you have not lost your mind," I said. "Edd, well, he's another story," I added with a chuckle.

She smiled and started to retell accounts she had told us previously. I didn't have a problem with this and I sat quietly listened. I knew she needed to talk. Most people having strange happenings in their home have no one or very few confidants they can trust. Often, they fear people they turn to will either think they're nuts or will want to tell about their own experiences. Beth needed neither; she needed someone to talk to openly without fear of being judged or interrupted. I also hoped she might reveal something she hadn't included in a previous telling.

She told me about seeing the woman in the bathroom doorway who told her, "It will be all right." This time, she added she and Edd were having a serious argument. She wondered if Edd's mother had stopped by to reassure her they would "be all right." I wondered if Edd had planted this theory in Beth or if she truly felt this was what may be happening. She also told me more about Emily and the effect all of this seemed to have on her.

"She used to talk all the time, babbling on about this and that," Beth said. "But after we moved here, like three months ago, she just stopped talking. Now she just whines or grunts and points to what she wants. I wish I knew why. And up until about a month ago she slept fine. Now almost like clockwork around one in the morning she wakes up screaming. She doesn't want a bottle and her diaper isn't wet or dirty, she just wakes up screaming."

Beth turned back to the TV and stared at it. I told her we would try to find out what exactly was going on in the house and help them in anyway we could, but of course there are no guarantees.

"At least you're here," she said. "I feel like I may get a good night's sleep too, for a change."

I handed her one of our two-way radios and showed her how to use it. I told her if anything happened just to give us a shout and we'd be there as quickly as we could. This seemed to make her feel better.

"Do you hear that?" Steve interjected.

Beth started laughing. "That's Edd. He snores like that when he's sleeping soundly."

"Does he always get that loud?"

"Give him a few minutes, it'll get worse," she said with a big smile on her face. "He says he doesn't snore at all. Even the boys have told him he does, but he doesn't believe them."

"Well now he'll have proof," I said. "The tape recorder will pick up every glorious moment of that for us to play back for him."

Beth laughed again and began turning the lights off.

"Do you need anything before I go to bed?" she asked.

"Nope, we're fine Beth," I replied. "Sleep well and use the radio if you need or want to. Okay?"

"Okay," she said before heading down the hall to her bedroom.

It was just after midnight. I turned the TV off. Steve sat in Edd's easy chair and stretched out his legs. Edd's snoring finally stop at 12:30 a.m. Steve and I joked Beth must have poked him hard enough to get him to turn over. The family's three pet cats found their places to snuggle up for the night. We waited. In the silent darkness, we waited and hoped for solid evidence there was something paranormal going on in this house. That's when we heard the dragging noise coming from the family room. Steve made it to the sliding glass doors before I even made it off the couch.

"Do you see anything? Can you tell where it's coming from?" I asked.

"No, nothing," he answered. "Let me open the door and see if I can still hear it in the room itself." As he slowly pulled open the sliding glass door a rush of cold air came through. "Did you feel that?" he said.

"Yes, is there an open window or something?" I asked.

"Not that I can see, let me check around," he replied.

I realized I hadn't grabbed the temperature gauge in my hasty *unassing* from the couch so I dashed back into the living room to retrieve it. I heard a woman's voice in the hallway. "Hey!" was loud and clear to me. I turned and saw Steve looking down the hall.

"Did you hear that?" I asked.

"I sure did. Sounded like a woman said 'Hey' to me," he said. "What did you get?"

"Same thing. I heard 'hey' in a feminine voice."

Ros's voice came over the radio, "Was that you guys?"

"Was what 'us guys?'" I replied.

"I just heard a lady talking," Ros answered. "Couldn't make out what she said clearly, but I know I heard a lady's voice."

"Nope it wasn't us."

"10-4."

We went through the rooms taking readings. Steve checked the family room for open or broken windows and found all closed and intact. He found no source for the dragging noise. The temperature was only a few degrees less than the rest of the house. I felt so stupid for not grabbing the temperature gauge. This would not happen again. From that moment on I would always keep an EMF, flashlight, pocketknife, temperature gauge and a camera with me at all times.

We found nothing remarkable until we returned to the hall. As we stood in the middle of the hall between the bathroom and Emily's room we heard distinct voices. It sounded like they were coming from the bookcase. I checked the bathroom and found nothing. Steve checked Emily's room and found nothing. There was a hot spot in front of the bookcase, 87 degrees in a house that averaged 75 degrees. I popped my head into Edd and Beth's room to see if they had left the TV or radio on and found they had not. We heard the dragging noise again. It was 1:00 a.m. When I turned to go back down the hallway Ros opened the door to the back bedroom. I almost jumped out of my skin.

"Did you hear that sound?" she asked. "It sounded like someone opened the sliding closet door, to me."

"We heard the 'dragging' noise; could that be what you heard?" I asked.

"No, this sounded like the closet door, but on the opposite wall. And look!" she exclaimed, pointing down the hall by the bathroom door. I turned to see a shadowy figure move from the bathroom across the hall into Emily's room.

"Steve, check Emily's room again," I shouted. "Check everything."

He nodded and just as he opened the door, Emily screamed. She stood on the far end of the crib closest to the door, screaming and pointing at the wall. Beth heard her over the baby monitor and was in the room within two minutes. She checked her diaper and found it was dry. Emily clung to Beth and kept crying and looking back at the wall where Ros had heard the strange sound. Beth decided to heat a bottle for Emily and left for the kitchen. Steve and I investigated the noise in the family room while Ros took readings of the back bedroom, hallway and Emily's room. When Steve and I finished our readings we went to help Ros. We were all standing in Emily's room when we felt a noticeable cold spot moving through the room. We first noticed it by the changing table then it moved past the crib, then by the closet before finally leaving the door into the hallway. The cold spot produced a reading of 52 degrees while the rest of the room was 74 degrees. We followed it out into the hallway and found Emily standing there looking towards it. It passed through the dinning area and into the family room. As it passed, Emily she began to cry again and ran to Beth who was still in the kitchen. Beth leaned down and picked her up to comfort her.

Steve checked the family room for readings and as he neared the back window, a single vertical blind started to move rapidly back and forth. We could hear the noise it made inside the house. I looked out the sliding glass door to see it turn straight out, move back and forth, then turn back flat against the other blinds before it came to a complete stop.

"That was weird," Steve said when he returned. All I could say was "Um, uh huh."

Emily was in the living room, refusing her bottle, so Beth and Ros tried to play with her. She suddenly climbed down off the couch and said, "Hmm, okay." She walked to the sliding glass door leading to the family room and stood there pointing and looking back at Beth. Beth walked over to her, put her arms around her and said, "Do you want your toy?" assuming Emily wanted her toy sitting in the flour. "No," Emily shouted, jerking out of her mother's comforting arms.

Steve got as close as he could without distracting Emily to take readings. I began taking photos of her as she stood at the glass doors talking to someone. Ros stood silently with an amazed look on her face and poor Beth looked back at us, confused. Emily said "It's right there, do you want to play with it? I'll help you."

She began hitting at the door trying to get into the family room.

Beth said, "No sweetie, you can't go out there. It's time for you to go back to bed."

Emily turned back towards the door and said, "Nite, Nite," before reaching up to Beth to carry her into her room. Beth returned Emily into her crib and laid her back down.

"Did that just happen?" Ros said.

"Which part of it?" Steve said, laughing. "If you mean did something wake the baby up and she recognized it and talked to it? Um, yes, I do believe that is what we just witnessed. Damn! That was too weird! I'd say if I didn't have you two to confirm it, I imagined the whole thing."

"I know what you mean dude, it was really strange. Emily saw or at least appeared to see whatever it was," Ros said.

"Well, there were definitely temperature fluctuations in the room while she was talking to whatever-it-was," Steve said. "Hopefully we caught something on the video or audio tape."

"Yeah, that would be nice," commented Ros.

"If Beth comes back out here, don't feed her fears," I said. "Let's try to downplay it some until we can figure out what the heck is going on in this house, okay? We don't want to scare these folks anymore than they all ready are. Keep a cool head about this."

Ros and Steve agreed as Beth returned.

"I'm going back to bed," she said. "Emily gets up pretty early. Good night again."

We all wished her a good night and sat looking at one another with raised eyebrows. Did she not see what had transpired? Was she too afraid to deal with it? Was she blocking it out? Or was she so used to this strange behavior it didn't mean anything anymore? Whatever the case she hadn't mentioned it before returning to bed.

Ros headed back to the small bedroom while Steve and I checked the audio and video tapes. We took our usual readings of all the rooms and nothing seemed out of the ordinary. No peaks on the EMFs, no temperature variations, nothing. All was quiet at 3:00 a.m. in the Dunnam house.

I settled back into my place on the couch taking notes on what we'd seen in the past hour. Steve took his place of vigil in Edd's easy chair, staring down the hallway. Every few minutes something would happen: the dragging noise from the family room, the sound of knocking on the wall behind Edd's easy chair, voices in the hallway, an occasional loud "thud" or "bang" sound. Every few minutes we'd hear a click sound. We would get up to find the source but find nothing. The EMF would get various readings. The thermal scanner would pick up fluctuations in the temperature, but no source of the sounds was found. The noises kept us hopping for the remainder of the early morning hours.

At 4:30 a.m., Ros's voice came across the radio, "Was that you guys?"

"What did you hear Ros?" I asked.

"I just heard a man moaning," she replied. "I'm coming out, be there in a sec." The back bedroom door opened and Ros emerged from the dark corridor. "That wasn't you in the hall Steve?"

"Nope, I've been sitting right here for about ten minutes," he replied.

"Describe what you heard Ros," I said.

"It was like a moaning sound, a man's voice from what I could tell," she said, "deep and long like this, 'mauauauauauahhhhhhh.' It was in the room I felt like someone was standing by the closet staring at me when it happened. Sorry dude, but I'm done in there for the night. Way too many noises and voices. I'm going to hang here with you guys for the rest of the night if you don't mind."

"I don't mind," I said. "I told you that before, I don't need you in there scared."

Steve jumped up and said, "I'll go sit in there for a while and see if anything happens."

"Cool, you can go in there with me while I collect my things," Ros said.

When Ros returned to the living room, she stretched out on the floor facing the sliding glass doors. I replaced Steve in Edd's easy chair. We continued to hear the now familiar sounds of voices, dragging, knocking, clicking, thuds and bangs.

Ros commented laughingly, "Maybe I was better off in the back bedroom, it was quieter in there." I laughed as I wrote notes in my journal. We both continued to seek for sources and take readings in the various locations.

It was nearly 5:30 a.m. when Steve emerged from the back bedroom.

"Anything?" I asked.

"I didn't get much," he reported. "I did hear the sound like the closet door was opening, but didn't get any corroborative data on any of the equipment and I couldn't figure out the source. Nothing in there should make that noise in that location. I checked the closet door and it made no noise when I opened it. The boys' closet is also diagonally opposite from where the sound comes from. The EMF and the temperature gauge acted like the batteries were dead. I put in fresh batteries, but they still didn't respond like they normally do."

"Hmm, make sure you note all of that in your log," I replied. "Did the area of the sound seem to correspond with the changing table in

Emily's room?"

"Yep," he replied.

"Hmm, interesting, maybe next time we should focus more on Emily's room and see what happens."

"Sounds like a plan," Ros said.

"Okay, let's start breaking down the equipment," I said. "Edd will be getting up soon and we should be ready to leave when he does."

We quickly broke down all of the equipment and made sure all the tapes were labeled with times, dates and location. We were sure to break off the tabs to prevent the tapes from being recorded over and carefully repacked the equipment into their cases.

I went into the family room to check on Emily's toy and found it had moved. It had rolled about five inches leaving a trail through the flour on the plastic bags. I noticed that while I had stood at the sliding glass door, I couldn't see the tracks in the flour. The line of sight angle was just so that unless I walked into the room and stood by the toy, I wouldn't have seen the tracks in the flour.

I called Steve and Ros in to see. Steve commented it looked like someone had held it down heavily while rolling it. The impression in the flour was deep, deep enough the center of the toy actually made a mark in the flour as well. Could this have been a part of the clicking noise we'd heard throughout the course of the night? Had the entity Emily had spoken to earlier played with her toy after she went back to sleep? Was this toy easier for an unseen visitor to move around? Or maybe they just liked the colors and sound the toy made when it did move. We came to find out this was not the only toy at the Dunnam house moved by unseen hands. I photographed the toy and the flour and cleaned up the bags. None of the flour had spilled onto Beth's carpet, so I didn't need to vacuum the room.

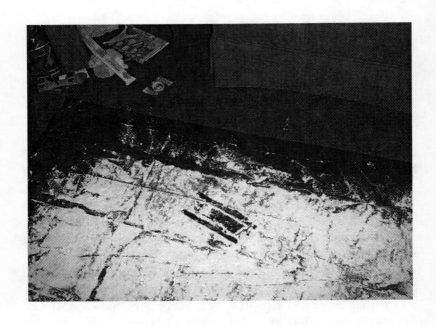

Ros had just zipped the last case closed when Edd came walking down the hallway.

"Morning gang!" He bellowed.

We all greeted him in our own exhausted way as he began to make his lunch. He was very awake for six o'clock in the morning. We were all very tired from our long event-filled night. He opened up a Coke and tossed some M&M's into his mouth as he watched us carry equipment cases out to the car.

"So Dusty, catch any ghosties last night?" he asked.

"I won't really know until we look at the video and listen to the audio Edd, but it was definitely an interesting experience," I replied. "And it does appear they like Emily's toy. It moved about five inches in the flour last night."

"Cool," he responded, laughing. "Interesting? Don't I know it. That's the first good night's sleep I've had in months. If for nothing else, I gotta thank you guys for that. And thank you for allowing me to feel like I'm not crazy, that this stuff is really happening."

"No problem Edd," I answered. "Hopefully, we can figure out what's going on here so you can get a good night's sleep every night."

"That would be great kiddo. I can't tell you how this is wearing on my nerves. And poor Beth is stuck here in the house with this shit all day long. Damn, I gotta get my ass in gear, I'm gonna be late for work."

"Yeah, we're heading out now too Edd," I answered. "I'll call you in a day or so and let you know if we got anything on the tapes. And we can set up a time for our next visit. I'd like to run video in more locations next time."

"Great, I'm looking forward to seeing what you got. This shit is so freaky. And any night is good for us. Just let me know when you can come back," he said.

"And remember Edd, if anything happens email me," I answered. "Call me or jot it down for me. Since I can't be here all the time, you guys are my eyes and ears, okay?"

"Sure thing kiddo," he said. "The little wifey handles all of that.

My handwriting sucks!"

We all laughed and said our farewells as we packed our tired bodies back into my car for the trip back to Daytona. We didn't say much on the ride home. I know I was trying to digest all the strange things we had just witnessed. We had worked plenty of cases before, but nothing like this. If this were truly paranormal in nature, I had a feeling we were in for an interesting and eventful ride.

Ros broke the silence, "Edd is too much. How can anyone be that hyper and active at that hour of the morning?" Steve and I laughed and agreed with her.

I asked, "So, what is you guys take on what happened last night?"

"I don't know about you guys, but that moaning really freaked me out," Ros exclaimed. "It was right there and so loud and clear. You know I don't scare easy, but that 'mauuuhhh' sound scared me."

"It's got me baffled," Steve added. "There was no locatable source for the sounds, cold spots or EMF readings. Nothing natural or manmade was causing it. I don't want to say the place is haunted, yet. But there is definitely something going on there that doesn't make sense."

"Did anyone else notice the lack of sound in Emily's room?" I asked.

"Yeah, like our voices didn't bounce off of anything, like the air was dead or something," Ros said. "I did notice that now that you mention it."

"Me too," Steve added. "Like any noise fell into a void or was absorbed by something. It was weird, but I did notice it too."

We fell silent for the remainder of the drive home. I wanted to stay up when we arrived to go over the data we'd collected, but I knew I'd be sharper with some badly needed sleep. Ros dozed off for part of the ride. Steve made notes and theories in his pad. I put the car on cruise control and thought about the events of the previous night, trying to get a perspective on the hows and whys this house seemed to have so much activity. Even if all three of the deaths associated with the house and surrounding area were somehow causing the activity, it didn't make sense. There were more than three voices coming from the hallway. At times there were more than three locations having activity at the same time. I would soon find the longer I worked this case, the less sense it would make.

Chapter Four:
Viewing the Documentation from our First Night

When I finally awoke from some badly needed sleep, I started the coffee and grabbed the digital camera. I never rely on the digital camera for proof, too many as yet unknown variables can figure into the equation of a digital photo. I do use the cameras and it's nice to have the LCD screen in the field to see instantly what the camera captures. But only if I have corresponding data from at least one other source, will I use digital photos as back up data. I learned very early on that a digital camera will pick up all sorts of anomalies that the human eye can't or won't. Since the data is questionable coming out of the gate, I can't use it as a sole piece of evidence in a case. I also know there are some researchers in this field that will disagree with me on that point, but they aren't working my cases.

Since this field has always been plagued by charlatans, hoaxsters and people looking to make a buck or a name for themselves, it is hard enough to get any evidence of paranormal activity we collect to be taken seriously. Even within the paranormal investigations community itself various branches differ on the *right way* or the *wrong way* a case should be worked. Some feel "sensitives" or psychics should always be used. Others feel relying on modern equipment is the most accurate way to provide evidence. And still others feel a combination of sensitives and technology is best. Someone once told me using a sensitive was an antiquated approach to the field. I understood their opinion, but I don't agree with it. If we all thought along those lines, we wouldn't be driving cars, using telephones or still sending various probes into space. I can only go by my training and my experience in the field. And I choose to use both sensitives and technology.

As I viewed the digital photos I noticed the house didn't seem quite as active photographically as it had on our first trip. We had some anomalies on the digital camera but they were nothing to write home about. I felt a bit discouraged as I continued to view photo after photo with no anomalies. At one point I thought our first trip produced the best of what we were going to get. Maybe we had experienced something that only occurred during the summer months and into fall; a residual haunting over for the remainder of this year? The deaths that occurred in and around the home did correspond with that time of year. Maybe it was over until next summer and the noises, voices and clicks were the last of what we would hear this year.

There were several orbs in various locations that did correspond to other data we collected, but the heavy mist was not present. There seemed to be fewer orbs present than on our first trip, then one photo caught my eye. In the field this anomaly is sometimes known as an "energy ribbon," an unusual anomaly still under debate in the paranormal investigations field. It is thought the ribbon of energy is a highly electrically charged field of movement containing spirit energy. This energy is believed to be a way some spirits move around our human plane of existence. But this is just a theory. We had photographed this type of anomaly in other locations, but at the Dunnam house, this location was in line with the rainbow over the roof. If you were to draw a line from the energy ribbon through the house, and another line from the rainbow down through the roof, the lines would intersect at the bookcase in the hallway. This showed some promise.

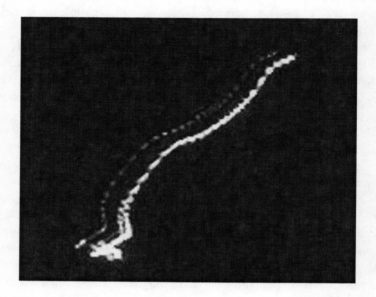

I finished my coffee and dropped the rolls of film off at Walgreen's photo counter and waited. This time the photo department wasn't very busy, so I thought I'd wander through the store to pick up a few things while I was waited. When my hour was up, I returned to the counter with an armload of fresh film, batteries, audio and video tapes to retrieve the prints. I returned home and anxiously ripped open the film envelopes, more disappointment. There were no anomalies on four rolls of 35-mm film.

My hopes were low when I began to view the first videotape taken in the family room. I grabbed my notepad and pen and settled in for the long session ahead of me. I normally like to have someone there to assist me, but it isn't always possible. The sometimes long periods of boredom can be eased with a companion. Watching a film of a closet door for four hours can get tiresome, especially if there are no anomalies to be seen or heard. It also helps to have extra eyes because one person may see something the other didn't. This time, Steve was there to help watch the footage. I hit the play button and was ready, pen in hand.

I tend to break a cardinal rule of video taped investigations. The rule states don't over tape an area, unless you're prepared to watch every minute of tape you record. We do watch every minute of tape, but, I tend to "over-tape" most locations since we overlap our views and cover a great deal of the area. It can be tedious and take a great deal of my time to view all this video, but it has proven well worth that time expenditure on more than one occasion. I was hoping our luck would hold out for this set of tapes.

As Steve and I focused on the TV, we waited for any possible results to emerge, either in a viewable or audible form. At 12:24 a.m. it began. We heard the same click sound we'd heard on the audio tape recorded in the back bedroom. I noted the click sound on my pad. During the next two hours we would hear 41 clicks. Some of the clicks were grouped in twos or threes while others were single. I made a note of each click or group of clicks along with the times they occurred. Steve and I discussed whether the clicks were caused by Emily's small toy. The sounds seemed to come from somewhere very close to the microphone on the surveillance camera. It could have been in the area where the toy was surrounded by flour since it was only about four feet away from the camera.

We continued watching and listening. We saw Ros standing at the breakfast bar but didn't capture her ball of light on tape. We saw Emily and Beth at the door while Emily held her conversation with unseen guests. We saw the cat jump up on one of the barstools at the breakfast bar, and then jump back down. The angle of the camera and the use of night vision worked out well enough to see when someone entered or left the living room area. Steve and I agreed we had an almost perfect shot covering a great deal of area of the four different rooms.

The tape continued. At 2:44 a.m., we saw Steve enter the family room to take readings and flip the audio-tape. He walked through the room with temperature gauge and EMF, obviously getting no significant readings as his note-taking was brief and his actions uneventful. As Steve bent over to flip the tape, a small bright ball of light appeared from behind the breakfast bar, looped around the kitchen, then passed through the closed sliding glass doors and shot straight across the family room between Steve and the camera. I hit the pause button on the VCR and said, "Did you see that?"

"I sure did," Steve replied. "Play it back."

We watched the same few seconds of tape over and over at least two dozen times while we reviewed our notes and discussed the possible causes of what we saw on the tape. We ruled out camera flash, lighting, cats, people, bugs and every other rational explanation that came to mind. Edd, Beth and Emily had been asleep in their rooms and Ros was still in the back bedroom. I had been sitting on the living room couch making notes with all three cats sleeping close by. Steve didn't have a camera with him. The only light was on over the kitchen sink and it couldn't be seen in the tape. A bug could not pass through solid glass. We concluded we indeed had something, what it was, we didn't know. But we agreed it was not caused by anything known to us; at least nothing natural or manmade. We also realized the overlapping camera views we had so carefully planned were useless for this piece of footage. None of the cameras had a clear shot into the kitchen: so much for our nearly perfect camera angle.

As Steve and I continue watching the tape, our hopes now raised considerably. We watched as Steve finished turning over the tape and speaking the time, date and location into the microphone. We both noticed his head turn very suddenly towards the ball of light as it streaked out of the view. He pulled out the temperature gauge and I quickly flipping through his notes, I found he had written the temperature had dropped nine degrees in the four minutes he was in the room. At 2:48 a.m., his EMF read 3.3. At that point his face on the video had an odd look. I've known Steve for many years and knew if I said anything about him "being scared" it would bruise his ego, so I checked his notes. Sure enough, he wrote that after feeling the coldness in the room, he felt like he was being watched. We watched him write down a quick note then leave the room quickly. When he closed the sliding glass door behind him he turned to stare back into the room for several seconds. It seemed to me he thought as long as the door was closed whatever was on the other side couldn't get near him. I chuckled to myself but felt bad for doing so. I knew the odd feeling in that room and I'd jumped more times than I care to mention in there during our investigation of the Dunnam house.

From 2:51 a.m. until 3:26 a.m. we counted 21 more clicks but no signs of any other form of activity. At 3:31 a.m. a fast moving ball of light, smaller than the first, circled near the kitchen cabinet above the stove. It then took a sharp downward turn and disappeared above the stove but below the cabinet. Steve and I again reviewed the anomaly several times, ruling out possible causes for what we had just seen. Again we had no rational explanation.

From 3:32 a.m. to 3:46 a.m. there were 11 more clicks on the audio portion of the videotape. At 3:49 a.m. the video showed interference. The entire picture was snowy in the center for nearly two minutes. This snowy interference was accompanied by three loud popping sounds. I checked our notes and found this was the same as one of the times we heard voices coming from the hallway. I didn't think the two events were connected, but couldn't be sure. Over the next two and a half hours, we counted 95 more clicks on the videotape. There was no pattern to the frequency, no consistency in the amount and no notable change in the audible level where the clicks were concerned. It was not only perplexing it was quite annoying. I don't like unanswered questions and this one was beginning to bother me. What was making this sound coming through so loud and clear on the video footage?

At 5:18 a.m. on the videotape we heard a child singing. We

couldn't see her, but we damned sure heard her. It was faint, like it was off in the distance somewhere, but it was definitely a female child singing. It was sweet and innocent but with an eerie undertone to it. I checked the collective notes and found that no one had heard any out of place sounds at this time. Ros's notes reflected she had done a 15-minute walk-through ending at 5:17 a.m. She had begun in the back of the hallway walking to the front of the house. The family room was her last stop before stopping to make her notes. There was no mention of a child singing anywhere in the house. I moved between the living room and kitchen during this time. Steve was in the back bedroom. Edd, Beth and Emily were all still soundly sleeping. Could this singing little girl be the one Emily had spoken to earlier? Was she the one playing with Emily's toy bee? Who was this child and why was she here at the Dunnam house? Or could it have been a simple case of a nearby child waking up early and near enough to the Dunnam house to be heard singing? I hoped we'd find an answer.

We watched the remaining 45 minutes of videotape, taking lots of notes. There were several more clicks, another noise sounding like a baby's rattle, one more instance of interference accompanied by the popping noise and at 5:59 a.m., we heard the dragging noise clearly. It sounded like a heavy object or body was being dragged across the room. I almost felt I was listening to an old horror film with the "drag dead body" sound effect inserted but without corresponding visible action. What I saw didn't match what I heard. It was a bit unnerving.

Just after the dragging noise the tape ended. It was 6:00 a.m. I tallied up the clicks and found during the six-hour time period there were a total of 195 recorded on the audio portion of the videotape. All I could think was 'What the heck was going on in that room?' Steve and I discussed possible causes, but we faced two challenges. One, we'd need to return to the Dunnam house to rule out certain things, like the vertical blind movement. And two, we'd need to take a closer look at Emily's toy bee, a lot closer look. Since the toy had apparently rolled five inches, would it click 195 times if we rolled it five inches? I hoped we'd soon find out.

Now I was becoming a bit more positive about viewing our other videotape and listening to the audio and digital audio recordings. I listened to the audio recording from the family room first, then the tape from the back bedroom. I don't like listening to EVPs before bed and it was starting to get late. I figured if I heard Ros's moaning man, I wanted that sound out of my head before I lay down for a good night's sleep. On the audio tape from the family room we got 195 clicks. Imagine that, I thought. I heard two separate rounds of pops corresponding to the times of the pops we heard on the videotape. The little girl singing came across much clearer on the audio tape. When the interference showed up on the videotape, we got static on the audio tape. It sounded like a strong gust of wind had blown across the microphone. Now we had what seemed to be corroborative data.

I listened to the tape from the back bedroom next and was almost thankful there were no results, not even Ros's "moaning man." She had begun the 90-minute tape at 1:30 a.m. Her moaning man didn't arrive until about 4:30. We must have missed him. Darn!

Now I could get a restful sleep without the sounds of "Mr. Moaning" stuck in my head. I put away my notes and turned in for the night. It didn't prove to be quite the restful a night as I'd hoped for. The clicks, pops and bright balls of lights plagued my mind throughout the course of the night. I got up several times to list things to check, and then tried again to sleep. I finally gave up around sunrise and got up to turn the coffeepot on to get my juices flowing. I needed to be sharp to watch the 8-mm video footage and listen to the rest of the audio we recorded.

I sat with my coffee, pen and note pad to watch the 8-mm footage on the living room TV. The field of vision was straight through the living room and down the hallway providing an excellent view of us walking around taking readings. It showed us setting up equipment, Beth putting Emily to bed, Edd going to bed, Ros entering the back bedroom for her vigil, and the cats walking through the house. At 1:00 a.m. there was a blurry rainbow on the tape. This corresponded to the time I stood in the hallway listening to voices and Ros reported seeing the shadowy figure move from Emily's room into the front bathroom. Since Ros and I were in the foreground, I used our heights to estimate the shape was about 5'8" to 5'10" and approximately two feet wide. The shape appeared in front of the bookcase before moving towards Emily's bedroom door and passing through her door. It returned through Emily's door, lingered in the hallway for about five seconds then moved across the hallway into the front bathroom. 'What the heck was this?' I thought a question that would become my mantra for the Dunnam case. It made no sense. If it were a spirit, why was it showing up on the video tape as a rainbow? If it were not a spirit, what would cause such an anomaly to appear at the exact time that we had seen the shadowy figure move in the exact same pattern we had witnessed? Why rainbows? The questions were beginning to pile up and I needed to find answers.

The bulk of the 8-mm tape was unremarkable with a few odd sounds I couldn't explain. But this weird rainbow had me stumped. Over the years I've had strange things appear on video, print and audio I couldn't explain. Many times, I've taken video tape and printed photos to people I know have a great deal of experience in interpreting recorded oddities. They have on occasion, rationally explained a supposed anomaly, so I decided to take the camera and tape to the shop of one of my local experts to get an unbiased opinion. While one of the technicians inspected the camera to check for technical problems, the owner watched the portion of the tape with the rainbow on it. After silently viewing the piece for nearly three dozen times, he leaned back in his chair and began the inquisition.

"Where was this shot?"

"In a private home," I answered.

"And it was a new tape?"

"Yep."

"Was there a thunderstorm?"

"Nope."

"Did you use the battery pack?"

"No, it was plugged into a surge protector and then directly into the wall."

"No mirrors on any of the doors in the hallway?"

"Nope."

"Hot out or should I say in when you took this?"

"Nope, very mild and low humidity."

"Any lights on that could bounce off of something metal?"

"Nope."

He played the tape in slow motion and pointed to the attic crawl space door.

"And this is?"

"It's the entry to the crawl space for the attic."

"Oh, okay…never mind," he said. "Watch here when I play it back at 2x slow."

I leaned in and stared at the TV to see what he saw. When the object passed back through Emily's door into the hall then into the bathroom, I saw it. It had human form. I could clearly see the head, shoulders, arms, legs and all movement of a human walking the short distance across the hallway. This was no longer questionable in my mind. I didn't have to squint and turn my head sideways to see the form. It was very clear at this speed. He rewound the tape to the beginning and I watched as the apparition came up out of the floor in front of the bookcase then actually looked around before beginning its movement around the Dunnam house.

"Okay, so in your opinion, was this some sort of interference? Or some technical issue with the camera? Possibly there was some glitch in the tape from the factory?" I asked.

"I've been doing video and photo editing for 33 years, and I'll be quite honest with you, I've never seen anything like this before," he said.

"So you have no theories? No educated guesses?"

He shrugged his shoulders and yelled to the technician, "Anything wrong with the camera?"

"Nope, it's up to factory specs on everything," a voice yelled back from another room. "Was there a problem?"

"No, no problem," my expert shouted back.

'No problem? No problem?' I thought to myself. There was a problem, just one that neither the video camera technician nor the expert could explain. He rewound the tape and pulled it out of his camera before glancing at the label and handing it back to me.

"You always use that brand?" he asked.

"Yes, I thought it was the best, especially for the work I'm doing."

"It is. Kind of expensive for you, but it is the best. I don't see anything wrong with the tape either. Mind if I ask what's going on?"

"Well, we've got a house with some activity. We're trying to figure out what kind and why. You know, the usual." I said, laughing.

"I'm no authority on what you do, but I'll tell you what's going on there. You've got a ghost," he replied, also laughing.

"Yeah, I'm starting to think we really do."

I thanked him for his time and opinion. As I left, I gave the technician a few bucks for checking the camera and headed back home.

On the drive home my mind was racing with questions and possibilities. Could we have stumbled onto an actual haunted house? Who was this "rainbow being" that walked across the hallway? Who was the little girl singing? Who was Emily aware of that we adults didn't perceive? I felt more background digging was needed. I hoped I could find something else to confirm the level of activity was real. Maybe some historical yellow fever epidemic or senseless slaughter of Native Americans had taken place in the area? Maybe the Spanish had an encampment nearby hundreds of years ago? I knew that this task would not be an easy one, if I could accomplish it at all.

I had to listen to the digital voice recording still, so that was how I spent my evening. I hoped for some results, but realized that we had all ready gotten our fair share from other equipment sources. We may not have gotten many positive photos from that night, but the video and audio were, in my opinion, very active.

The following is the exact transcript of the results from the digital voice recorder from November 7 and 8 in the Dunnam house hallway.

DIGITAL VOICE RECORDER—EVP—DUNNAM HOUSE—11-7/8-2001—HALLWAY—2:18 a.m.–3:58 A.M.

2:21:28–2:21:45 a.m. MUFFLED SOUND
2:21:54 a.m. MUFFLED SOUND
2:22:03 a.m. MUFFLED SOUND
2:22:09 a.m. MUFFLED SOUND
2:22:31 a.m. MUFFLED SOUND
2:22:41 a.m. MUFFLED SOUND
2:23:06 a.m. MUFFLED SOUND
2:23:40–2:23:44 a.m. MUFFLED SOUND
2:25:16 a.m. MUFFLED SOUND
2:25:22 a.m. MUFFLED SOUND
2:25:30 a.m. HEAT CAME ON
2:28:30 a.m. HEAT SHUT OFF
2:28:35–2:28:39 a.m. VOICES
2:28:48–2:28:52 a.m. MUFFLED SOUNDS
2:29:16 a.m. MUFFLED SOUND
2:29:24–2:29:25 a.m. "HEY" SPOKEN IN A FEMININE VOICE
2:30:26–2:30:28 a.m. MUFFLED SOUND
2:30: 34 a.m. MUFFLED SOUND
2:32:19–2:32:26 a.m. "HEY, WHAT ARE YOU DOING" IN A MUFFLED MALE VOICE
2:32:29 a.m. MUFFLED SOUNDS
2:32:58–2:33:07 a.m. MUFFLED SOUNDS
2:33:36–2:34 a.m. BANG…"WHAT, WHAT"
2:33:01 a.m. "HEY" THUD SOUND
2:34:29 a.m. BANG
2:35:05 a.m. KNOCK
2:35:19 a.m. PUKING SOUND
2:35:26 a.m. TAPPING, LAUGHING
2:35:27 a.m. "NOW"
2:35:44 a.m. "MORE"
2:35:52 a.m. VOICE
2:36:07 a.m. MUFFLED SOUND

2:37:13 a.m. MUFFLED SOUND
2:38:17–2:38:20 a.m. DRAGGING SOUND
2:40:39 a.m. TAPPING
2:40:38–2:40:43 a.m. "HEY," TALKING
2:44:20 a.m. KNOCK
2:44:47 a.m. TAPPING
2:45:13 a.m. "WHAT"?
2:45:57 a.m. MUFFLED SOUND
2:50:58 a.m. VOICE
2:51:20 a.m. HEAT COMES ON
2:59:20 a.m. HEAT GOES OFF
3:01:21 a.m. MUFFLED SOUND
3:03:46 a.m. TAPPING
3:04:20 a.m. "I WANT YOU"
3:05:19 a.m. MUFFLED SOUND
3:08:48 a.m. KNOCK
3:10:54 a.m. MUFFLED SOUND
3:14:46–3:14:57 a.m. VOICES MUFFLED KNOCK
3:16:08 a.m. HEAT COMES ON
3:22:20 a.m. HEAT GOES OFF
3:23:44 a.m. MUFFLED SOUND
3:24:04 a.m. MUFFLED SOUND
3:24:15 a.m. MUFFLED SOUND
3:27:28 a.m. TAPPING
3:29:30 a.m. MUMBLING "AAGH" VOICE
3:31:33 a.m. KNOCK
3:38:12 a.m. MUFFLED SOUND
3:38:34 a.m. HEAT COMES ON
3:44:50 a.m. HEAT GOES OFF
3:45:08 a.m. BREATHING OR DRAGGING MUFFLED SOUND
3:48:48 a.m. TAPPING
3:49:07 a.m. TAPPING
3:49:50 a.m. TAPPING
3:50:22 a.m. TAPPING
3:50:58 a.m. VOICE

3:51:56 a.m. BANGING, LOW, MUFFLED
3:52:38 a.m. TAPPING
3:53:00 a.m. BANG
3:56:06 a.m. MUFFLED SOUND
3:56:54 a.m. LOUD BANG
3:58:02 a.m. DRIP

This was too much! I sat watching that hallway for several hours during our overnight at the Dunnam house, and even though I heard a few things, I know I didn't hear all of this! Some of the voices were so clear, it was amazing. The sound of someone puking and the maniacal laughter really unnerved me. I guess that's what gets under my skin with EVPs. Knowing something or someone is speaking or making noise right in front of you and you are unaware of them or unable to hear them. Then when you listen to the recordings and hear it all, it is very eerie.

The best piece of evidence was the female voice saying, "Hey" at 2:29 a.m. We all heard it and now it was also recorded at the time we heard it. Who was this woman? Was it Edd's Mother? Or maybe the woman that died in the Dunnam house? I wanted to know, but was tickled pink we caught this particular EVP at the corresponding time the three researchers reported hearing it with their own ears.

It is thought spirits can communicate audibly, but they sometimes use a sound frequency lower than the human ear can normally hear. That's why we use recording devices. They pick up what we can't or won't hear. Magnetic tape and digital recorders are the best in my opinion. Digital voice recorders are better to use than regular audio recorders because they have no motor noise to contaminate the recording. Digital technology eliminates the need for mechanical movement. If we do use mechanical tape recorders, we always run a test recording to identify the sounds made by the mechanism. I had one recorder that made a heartbeat sound as the tape neared the end. The first time I heard it *my* heart almost stopped.

I again began to question why. Why so much activity? Who or what was the source of it all? Why did it seem to be emanating from the hallway, specifically near the bookcase? I wrote a reminder note to ask where the bookcase had come from before beginning the long and tedious process of correlating the data. There was a great deal of investigation remaining to do at the Dunnam house and I felt we were up to the task. I hoped that if nothing else, we could help this family understand what was going on so they would be able to live in their own home without fear.

Chapter Five:
Waiting for the Holidays to end!

By the time I finished correlating all the data from our first overnight at the Dunnam house, less than two weeks remained until Thanksgiving. I spoke with Edd and Beth via emails and telephone about our findings. They both seemed very relieved they were not going crazy. Because the holidays were upon us, and we both had family coming into town, we agreed to stay in touch and the group and I would return after Christmas. They agreed to keep me informed of any occurrences either by email, phone and to keep a journal. I reminded them to call anytime, day or night, if they needed to do so. I had a feeling that I would be receiving lots of phone calls and emails over the next few weeks and my hunch proved correct.

Just two short days later I received an email from Beth with several photos from Halloween night she'd taken with a disposable 35-mm camera. Emily looked adorable in her little cow costume, but there were some unexpected trick-or-treaters in the photos as well. There were several photos in the yard and out on the sidewalk that contained orbs, but one in particular struck me. Not only were there orbs inside the house, but there seemed to be some sort of face in the storm door looking at Emily. There were no bushes, trees or other obstructions, or even anything reflective hanging on the walls of the house that could have caused this odd face to appear in the door. For the first time on this case, my blood ran cold.

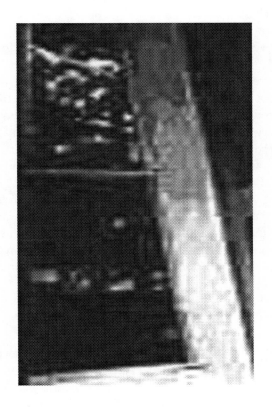

Above is a cropped out close up of the "face"
in the doorway of the Dunnam home.

This would prove to be the first in a long string of photos, phone calls and emailed sound events I received from the Dunnams throughout the holiday season. Since we weren't planning an onsite investigation during this time, it gave me time needed to further explore the history of the house and grounds, and to contact a few of my peers for some desperately needed advice and guidance. I rolled up my sleeves and got busy. I spent hour upon hour sifting through old records, maps and obituaries in both Volusia and Seminole County. Several trips to the government records offices, libraries and historical societies turned up little usable information. I finally found a map from the late 1500's showing the area that is now Deltona. This map was made by the Spanish troops during their first occupation of Florida. The map showed a large Native American settlement and a small Spanish fort to the southwest of the settlement. I began to wonder if the Dunnam home had been built on sacred Seminole lands. Or had there been a battle with the Spanish over this land? I phoned a friend of mine in south Florida who is a member of the traditional Seminole Nation and spoke with him about the possibilities. He reminded me that a short distance away from the Dunnam home is where Chief Osceola and his soldiers were captured. So, the possibility of a battle of some sort was very high. He told me he'd check on the portion of the land in question and get back to me with what he could find out.

"No promises though," he added.

My next and thankfully smaller project was to contact a few folks I respect in the paranormal field. I typed out an email giving the high points of the case. I expressed my fears, concerns and theories and asked for any advice, guidance or direction that they could give me to help this family. I sent this email to Troy Taylor, with the American Ghost Society; Dave Juliano, with Shadowlands, The Light and the South Jersey Ghost Research; and Dave Oester, with the International Ghost Hunters Society. Troy Taylor replied first. He told me he'd never experienced the activity we reported experiencing, but suggested I contact renowned psychic Kelly Weaver to see if she might be able to *see* the cause of the events. I next heard from Dave Juliano. He gave me some great advice on how to help the family better deal with the activity. But one word glared out from his email to me, "demonic."

I train my researchers to never use the "d" word, demon. It sets up a psychological turmoil within the family that cannot be undone easily. We also never use the "e" word, "evil," for the same reasons. We use such terms as "non-human negative energy." It implies the same thing, but most people don't have as hard a time wrapping their mind around the term as they do "evil demon." I didn't want to even think about this possibility. I had read about demonology and several cases worked by pioneers in the field, but I did not want to consider this possibility. I sat at my computer for seemingly hours reading and rereading Dave's email. I printed it out, read it again and then placed it in the growing Dunnam case file.

I then emailed Kelly Weaver and asked for her help. I gave her no information that would be leading in anyway. She quickly replied, asking for three 35-mm photos containing no positive results, no family members or no personal information. At first I thought this task would be nearly impossible but after I flipped through the photos I realized it was easy. I found one photo of the hallway, one showing the front of the house with the address not showing and one of the family room. I mailed them to Kelly the same day. I never heard back from Dave Oester, which left me with a foul taste in my mouth. Dave Oester was always ready to take money from me for courses, books, CD's and the like, but was never there when I needed advice. Although I remain a member of the IGHS, I personally don't like doing business that way.

The first telephone call from the Dunnam family came in two days before Thanksgiving. Edd called to wish everyone a Happy Thanksgiving. He told me the sounds continued; voices, singing, footsteps and the dragging noise from the family room. He said they had now begun to hear a child's voice singing through the baby monitor early in the morning. At first Beth thought it might be Emily, but soon realized it was not. This had occurred half a dozen times since we had last been at the home. It happened after Edd left for work, but before Emily had awakened. Twice it happened when the monitor was completely turned off. Beth described it as being both "sweet and sad." I knew exactly what she meant. I had heard the child's voice singing on the audio tape, a sweet innocent voice sounding so lost.

The next contact was an email from Beth, very concerned about Emily. One of the unseen guests at the house was not only playing with her toys and talking to Emily, but Emily now seemed to prefer to spend more and more time alone with her unseen "friend." Emily had begun to share food, toys and many conversations with this unseen and uninvited guest. I called Beth to ask her if she wanted us to return earlier to see if we could find anything new.

"No," she said, "it has actually been quieter than before. No need to make the trip so close to the holidays."

"I will if you need me," I answered. "I know how worried you are. Especially about Emily."

"I know," she replied. "You have been great! I think we would have lost our minds if we didn't have you stopping by and able to call and talk to about this whole mess. Let's plan on something after Christmas, okay? Besides my family will be here tomorrow and we haven't told them anything yet."

"I understand," I said. "Let's get together after your family leaves. But remember, if anything happens, day or night, do not hesitate to call me, okay? And try not to worry."

"I will Dusty, I promise," she said. "You have a great holiday and we'll see you soon."

After the telephone call, I began to feel Beth's concern. Although the home didn't seem dangerous, just seriously annoying, I knew I wouldn't have my children to stay in that house. Many have agreed with me. Sometimes it's hard being a researcher. I empathize with the families, but it is not my place to tell them how to live their lives, I can only offer options. But Edd and Beth's options were limited. They had signed a lease and like many of us, were living from paycheck to paycheck. With a toddler, two teenage boys and a new baby on the way soon, their budget was stretched. There was no way they could afford to move on a limited income. Whatever was occurring in the house needed to stop so they could try to regain a normal family life.

I didn't hear from the Dunnams for another two weeks. I assumed Edd and Beth were busy with holiday preparations and Beth's visiting family. But you know what happens when you assume something? It tends to make an "ass" out of "u" and "me." No one seems to know why, but activity seems to increase during the holiday season, birthdays and anniversaries. It struck me as odd that this was not happening at the Dunnam house. I next heard from Edd in a Dec. 17 email bearing the subject line "Merry Christmas."

Edd wrote on the previous Thursday, he and Beth heard Emily crying at about 6:15 a.m. Edd, already half-awake, told Beth to stay in bed, he would check on Emily. He found her diaper needed changing, so he began the process. Emily seemed to be in a particularly bad mood, not normal for her mornings. As Edd attended to his daughter on the changing table and tried to calm her, he noticed she looked towards the bedroom door and started to laugh. Edd wrote he paused, not really wanting to turn around to see who or what may be behind him, but curiosity or fear finally got the best of him and he slowly turned. He said he saw what he described a man-sized dark figure staring into the room at them. The figure stood there for several seconds before turning away and moving down the hallway towards the master bedroom. Edd wrote he screamed for Beth "like a 12-year-old girl" as he grabbed Emily and ran out into the hall. As he turned on the hall light, Beth emerged from the master bedroom. When he described what he had just seen, he wrote Beth called him a "chicken shit," upset with him for waking her up. After all, the three most important things to a pregnant woman are sleep, food and bathrooms, she had told him. This name would eventually stick to Edd like glue. From that day forward he would be known as Edd "Chicken-shit" Dunnam. I even made him an honorary member of the research group, and had that name printed on his I.D. badge.

He briefly added a new annoyance for them which sounded like heavy footsteps, even a horse, walking back and forth on the roof at night. I saw both of these new events as examples of increased activity and wondered just how immune they had become to it all. He closed the email with well wishes for the holidays for the entire research group and joked how things had quieted down a bit but still kept him on his toes.

I knew I would need to head over near Deltona to finish some holiday shopping, so I decided to pay the Dunnam family a surprise visit. I would bring a few small gifts for the family and hopefully visit with them quietly for a while. And of course, I'd bring some equipment along, "just in case."

I packed up the Gauss meter, 35-mm camera, thermal scanner and a digital camera. I grabbed a case containing a VCR, a night vision surveillance camera and two audio recorders. I hoped Beth would let me leave them and make recordings for us every night. I made sure I had plenty of blank VHS and audio tapes in case she'd agree. I packed up the gifts and my journal and headed out the door. As I was finishing up shopping I realized my thoughts weren't very focused on gift-giving, they were focused on the Dunnam house. I'm told I am very good at purchasing the right gift for the right person, but that changed that holiday season.

I pulled up in front of the Dunnam home at about 8:30 p.m. I noticed lights were on, but only Edd's work van was in the driveway. I stuck the Gauss meter in one pocket, the 35-mm camera in the other, grabbed the bag of gifts along with the journal and walked towards the house. Just as my foot hit the concrete porch slab I heard a load thumping sound coming from the roof. I paused for a moment and backed up so I could see the entire roof and looked up. I saw nothing, but still heard the loud thumping noise. Edd was right, it did sound like a horse or very heavy man was walking back and forth across the roof. I grabbed the camera and snapped a picture in the direction of the sound. I clicked the Gauss meter on and it whined away with a 4.5. Below is the photo from over the garage area of the house.

A vehicle approached and I realized it was Edd and Beth. As the van pulled into the driveway, the Gauss meter went silent and the thumping sound stopped. I didn't mention this as they exited the vehicle. Edd stepped out of the van with a hearty, "Dusty! Hey kiddo, what are you doing here?"

"Hey Edd," I replied with a smile. "I was in the neighborhood and thought I'd stop by to wish you guys a merry, merry. Hey Beth. Hi Emme."

"Hi Dusty," Beth said as she grabbed Emily from the car seat. "Come on in, it's getting a bit chilly out here. Can you stay for a few minutes?"

"Sure I can. Need any help over there?"

"No, I've got her, but thanks," she replied. "Edd, get the bags and her sippy cup for me."

"I'm on it Mama," said Edd as he reached into the van and grabbed two armloads of grocery bags while trying to balance the sipper cup.

"Edd, let me help you with some of that," I said.

"Nah, I got it, but thanks. Get yer ass in here girl, we have some shit to tell you."

"Well at least let me get the door for you," I said, holding open the screen door while Beth unlocked and opened the front door. She carried Emily inside and sat down before beginning to remove layers of clothing from her sleepy child. Beth then grabbed a baby bottle from the kitchen and carried Emily to the child's bedroom.

"I'll be right back Dusty," she said over her shoulder. "Make yourself at home."

"Take your time Beth, I'm not going anywhere," I answered.

Edd finally made his way to the front door as I held it open for him

"Thanks kiddo!" he said as he maneuvered his way through the doorway with all the bags.

He placed the bags on the floor just to the side of the hall entryway. He then stood up and put his hands on his lower back as he arched his back. "Man! I'm sure glad that's over with! I am getting old," he said, groaning.

"Old? Come on Edd, you're younger than me by nearly a decade," I replied. "You're just suffering from the middle aged Rice Krispies."

"What the hell does that mean?" Edd asked.

"You're starting to snap, crackle and pop more often than when you were in your twenties," I said. We both laughed.

"By the way, where are Beth's parents?" I asked.

"They're out finishing some shopping and going to dinner with friends," Edd answered. "They'll be back soon."

"Well, maybe I shouldn't stay too long," I said. "I don't want you to explain to them who I am when they get back."

"Nah, we all ready told them all about you, had to. The voices, footsteps, noises and all where keeping them up at night."

"I was afraid that might happen," I said as Beth returned into the room. "Hey Beth, where did you get this bookcase from?" I asked.

"It's the landlord's, she answered. "He left it when he moved out. Why?"

"No reason, it's just an interesting bookcase," I said. "It looks as if it came out of a library or office of some sort."

"Give us a minute to put this stuff away and then we'll sit and chat," Beth said before turning to Edd. "Edd get Dad's golf clubs out of the living room for me please."

"No problem Beth, need any help?" I said.

"No, we're fine. Edd! The golf clubs."

"I'm on it Mama," Edd said as he lifted a half-full golf bag and headed toward the family room. I watched as he set it on the floor, the top resting steadily against an ottoman. He checked to make sure it wouldn't fall over before walking to the kitchen to help Beth unpack the groceries. I stepped into the living room and made notes in my journal, not wanting to tell Edd and Beth about my experience prior to their arrival. After I finished my notes, I closed my journal and tucked it into the waistband of my pants. Just then, Emily's little bee lit up and began to move. The bee stopped and turned off, then started off with another round of lights, sounds and movement across the living room floor. I must have had a look of disbelief on my face as Edd rounded the corner from the kitchen. Laughing, he said, "You'll get used to it Dusty."

I again thought to myself, "used to it?" There would be no way I could get used to this in my own home. But then, it wasn't happening in my home. If it were, maybe I would get used to it.

Edd blurted out in his animated way, "Merry Christmas to all the ghosties!" As soon as the words left his lips, he and I watched the set of carefully-placed golf clubs leap off the floor and slam into the door frame by the sliding glass door. I stood there looking at them like they were going to get up and dance when I heard something fall in the kitchen. As I turned to see what it was, I suddenly had the wind knocked out of me. All I remember is Edd asking me if I was okay and me doubling over, holding my left side. It felt as though I'd been hit with a baseball bat. I could hardly breathe. Apparently the golf clubs had indeed decided to dance for me, right into my rib cage! I would later discover three of my ribs were broken.

"Guess they don't like golf," Edd quipped.

"Or maybe they don't like Christmas," I replied.

I returned to the family room. Edd grabbed some ice for me as I turned the Gauss meter on. It whined away at a steady 3.8. The air temperature was cold, but only around the area of the golf clubs. There was a smell on the air, something like hot copper. The bag of clubs had struck the doorframe so hard they actually left an indentation mark in the wood molding.

"Hey Edd, you got a measuring tape?" I asked.

"Of course I do," he answered. "Hang on a sec, I'll get it."

When he returned with the measuring tape I asked him to hold one end over the golf clubs while I placed the other end on the floor where they originally lay. I did a double take when I saw the measurement, 5'4." What the hell was going on here, I thought. I tried to figure out if the clubs could have traveled that distance by falling and maybe rolling. But I could find no way they could have moved that distance, especially since they left the indentation in the molding not to mention the indentation in my side. I had witnessed the golf bag flying through the air and so did Edd. Then there was the fact a bag of clubs smashed into my ribs. I'm only 5'2" tall, but they still had to leap at least three feet off the floor to hit me as they did. Something in this house was definitely not happy with these clubs, Edd's comment about Christmas or maybe something else. Maybe it was my presence that had stirred them up. After all, Beth had said things had been quieter. And now this.

This was the first real physical assault I had experienced. Up until now, I've had hair pulling, feet stomped on and the occasional pinch, smack or punch. Those were tolerable, but this was over the edge even for me. My experience to date had not prepared me for this magnitude of activity. Would it ever, I thought to myself.

A line from the movie *Poltergeist* suddenly pierced my mind. "I don't know what hovers over this house, but it was strong enough to punch a hole into this world…" I stopped myself from finishing the line. The thought of this activity physically harming Emily or the boys was more than I wanted to deal with emotionally. But this was no movie. It was really happening in these nice people's home. Not that I feel Hollywood has made my job any easier, but the writers do afford this field with some memorable and often funny lines to use. Though, this line was one I never wanted to be able to use and definitely not funny.

It was time to make a decision. The team could return, night after night, to record data. Or the family would need to begin a daily ritual of removal and protection work that might stop the activity from recurring. I asked Edd and Beth to sit with me in the living room to discuss their options. This was no longer the Friday night cocktail party joke the family once thought it was; this situation was obviously becoming dangerous. What if one of the children, young Emily, was standing in the path of those golf clubs? She could have been seriously injured. I don't think a doctor would believe a ghost was involved in the injuring her. These are the kinds of thoughts and emotions that tear a family apart in a house that has negative activity. I could see the personality changes beginning in both Edd and Beth. Edd was less jovial and seemed obsessed with the activity. Beth had begun to withdraw further and further from everyone. I knew further changes would occur if this activity remained unchecked.

As we discussed the situation and the options, I told Beth of some generally accepted methods for helping to protect her family. Since she would be home most of the time, it would become her job to ensure these rituals were performed regularly. She would need to burn white candles every night and establish rules for her uninvited guests and stick to them. One of the best practices to keep activity in check is to say "Be good, or be gone!" out loud any time something happens. Just say it out loud, I explained. I added it would feel odd or weird to say it the first few times, but they would get used to it. It had worked in cases we'd worked in the past.

I explained burning incenses can aid in the protection process as well. Burning a combination of Frankincense and Myrrh or White Sage is most effective. Since they had no strong Christian beliefs,

Holy Water would have little effect. If the person using the protective item believes in its power to protect, then it will. If they don't have faith, it won't. The power of the mind is an incredible thing. With everything going on in the house, I wanted and needed them to use something believed strongly would work. Another problem is that if this activity was associated with a human spirit, the spirit may not be that of a departed Christian. Using Holy Water on someone who may have been a Buddhist wouldn't work. I thought it was best to stick with what worked in most cases.

Then I had to drop the bombshell. I told them after they began all this work; the activity might even increase for a time. Worst of all, it may never stop completely. They both got very quiet and for the first time, I saw the fear on their faces. Beth finally broke the long silence and said she would go shopping the next day, Christmas Eve, to buy some candles and incense.

"I would also like to set up the night vision surveillance camera and leave you with an audio recorder," I said. "I can show you the buttons to push to start them. Just let them run until the tapes finish. This may give me more insight into what is going on when I'm not here. Do you feel up to this Beth?"

"Sure," she replied. "Just show me what to do. I'm up half the night with bathroom breaks anyhow. And if it helps in some way, I'd be glad to do it."

"Great," I said. "Let me run out to the car and get the equipment. Be right back."

I grabbed the equipment from my car and dragged it back towards the house. As I got to the front porch Edd opened the screen door for me and took one of the cases from my hands. I unpacked the audio recording equipment first. I ran the 16-foot microphone cord up the wall and past the bathroom so the microphone hung directly across from the bookcase. I moved the recorder around the corner into the living room against the wall so no one would kick it or trip over it accidentally. I taped the recorder and the microphone wire down for safety reasons. I pulled out three blank tapes and showed Beth how to mark them with date, time and location. I then showed her how to turn on the tape recorder and how to operate it.

She smiled and said, "That's simple, no problem."

"I'd like to set up the surveillance camera in Emily's room, since that's where she and Edd saw the shadowy figure, but she's sleeping, right? I don't want to make noise and wake her," I said.

"We can sneak in and set it up, she sleeps like a log," Edd answered.

As I started to say, 'Okay, I'll be as quiet as I can,' we heard Emily begin to cry. Edd and Beth leaned towards her bedroom door to hear if she might just fall back asleep when we heard another voice came through the baby's bedroom door. It was a feminine voice, almost comforting. "Shh...Be quiet," the voice said. "Shh...Be quiet," it repeated.

Edd burst into Emily's room with Beth close behind him. I was right behind. Emily was standing up in her crib crying and pointing to the closet door. Beth grabbed Emily and left the bedroom. Edd walked straight over to the area in front of the closet where Emily had been pointing. He motioned for me to come over to the spot where he stood. It was freezing! We could both see our breath. An area of about five feet in diameter was ice cold. I stepped in and out of the cold spot several times and it finally began to warm. The hair on the back of my neck stood up. I had goose bumps all over me and they weren't from the cold. I noticed there was still no echo in the room. I thought of Edd's description of the shadowy figure, but Edd described the figure he saw as being male. This voice was clearly feminine. What the hell was going on here," I thought. Just how many spirits were in this house? And why were they here? The cold spot finally warmed to the ambient room temperature. Edd just stood there looking angry and confused. I told him to go into the living room to see if Beth needed comforting or help with Emily and I would set up the camera and VCR.

"Yeah, okay, I think I need to sit for a minute," he said.

I set the camera onto the tripod and placed it on the shelving directly across the room from the crib and doorway. I finished making all the connections and ran a test with the monitor to make sure the angle of the camera was correct. I adjusted the camera and was finally satisfied with the shot. I wrote the information on a new video tape and hit the record button. After collecting my garbage and leaving two more new blank tapes on top of the VCR, I returned to the living room to talk with Edd and Beth again.

"Are you okay Beth?" I asked.

"Yeah," she answered. "I just don't understand why all of this is happening to us."

"Neither do I," I said. "But let's stick to the plan and get it to stop. Okay?"

"That would be nice," she said. "To be able to sleep at night with no fear or noises, to not worry about the kids and what's going to happen next. I hope this does work."

"It should, just keep the faith and get into the routine of doing what I told you every night," I said. "All you have to do in Emily's room is put a new tape in each night and hit the record button. Mark the tapes the same way as I showed you with the audio tapes, and let it run all night. Is Emily all right? She looks pretty cozy now."

"Yeah," Beth answered. "She cried for a few minutes and kept looking back at her bedroom, but the warm bottle put her right back to sleep."

"By the way, do you mind if I borrow Emily's bee?" I asked.

"Not at all. It's right there on the floor next to Edd. May I ask why?"

"I want to record the noise it makes when it rolls; just another of my silly experiments.

"Sure. Anything you need Dusty," Beth said.

"I also want to check on something in the family room. Do you mind?"

"Not at all."

"Need some help kiddo?" Edd asked.

"Sure Edd. I could use an extra hand, if Beth doesn't need you for a few minutes."

Edd and I went into the family room and I pulled an audio recorder from my bag of tricks. I turned it on and began shaking the vertical blinds. I would shake each one from left to right, then from right to left. I tried making noise with them by pulling and pushing on them towards and then away from the windows. Edd kept looking intently at me and I felt he thought I was the crazy one in this house. I took two and three of the vertical blinds and repeated the same movements as I did with the single blinds. I twisted them to hear and record the sound that movement made. I needed this data to compare to the audio results we had gotten from our last visit. When I explained this to Edd, he nodded in approval.

Edd and I returned into the house and stood at the bar in the kitchen. As I wrote notes in my journal, he asked a few polite questions about my preparations for the holidays. As I set my pen down, that's when it hit me, literally! Within seconds something pulled my hair, stomped on the top of my left foot and hit me in the stomach. The punch to my stomach was so hard I nearly lost my breath. Edd reached over and grabbed my upper arm to steady me and asked if I were all right. I felt stupid as I stood there on one foot hunched over a bit, my right hand and arm across my abdomen.

I finally stood upright, placed my hands on my hips and spoke in a loud voice, "All right you guys! That will be quite enough of that kind of behavior! You will all be good, or you will all be gone."

Beth entered the kitchen and looked horrified I dared to challenge whatever it was that had hit me. "Is that what you mean Dusty?" she asked. "Tell them like that?"

"You bet Beth," I replied. "It's your house. Just like you would set rules for your children, set rules for them. Be firm about it, but not mean."

"Wow! Okay, I can do that."

"Well, I'd better get going, it's getting late," I said, trying to close the conversation.

"When can you come back?" Beth asked.

"Is the 26th all right for you?"

"Sure."

"Edd? Take a walk out back with me real quick before I leave?" I asked.

"Sure thing kiddo. Let me grab my jacket," Edd answered.

Edd and I walked into the backyard together. Edd remained silent, unusual for him. I began snapping photos with the 35-mm camera and finally asked, "Edd? Are you all right?"

"Yeah, just digesting all of this," he replied. "I want to protect my family, but trying to protect them from whatever this is, is nearly impossible. I feel helpless for the first time in my life."

"I can understand that Edd," I counseled. "Just stay strong for them and do the things we talked about in the house. Eventually this will all work out."

I really couldn't think of anything else to say that would be of more comfort to him. I now felt helpless too. I knew I would need to get more advice from people with more experience than I with this type of activity. I would email Dave Juliano again in the morning and hope that Kelly Weaver got back to me with her impressions.

Edd and I walked back toward the front of the house. I popped my head in the door to wish Beth a good night. She walked to the door and gave me a hug. Edd walked me to my car and hugged me as well.

"Try not to worry Edd," I said as I opened my car door. "One way or another we'll get this mess worked out. I'm here for you, day or night and until the end."

"Thanks Dusty," he said. "I really don't know what we'd do if you guys weren't coming down here and if we didn't have you to talk to. This shit is too crazy. It's starting to wear on my nerves."

"Edd, you don't need to thank me. It's my job. I should be thanking you and Beth for how nice and helpful you both always are when we come over. We are intruding on your lives."

"Better you and your gang than what's in the house Dusty," he returned.

"I guess you're right there Edd. Try to have a Merry Christmas, just focus on that and visiting with Beth's family. If not for you, do it for Emily. Make sure Beth takes care of her new tasks and try not to worry. I'll see you again in two days. Call if you need me, okay?"

"You got it kiddo. Merry Christmas," he added as he closed my car door for me.

I saw the look of concern on his face as he waved to me when I began to pull away from the house. I looked back at the house and saw Beth still standing at the door also looking concerned. It was heart wrenching to drive away that night.

My mind raced with thoughts of what had occurred during my short visit as I drove home. The concerns of this family were now my concerns as well. I realized on that drive how hard it is to disconnect from a case. There is no removal of emotions when you see, hear, feel and smell what a family is experiencing. Although I can remain objective with data, my empathy is not something I can just shut off. I have learned to hide it in most cases, but this case was making it harder and harder for me to avoid being a Mommy to Emily, a sister to Beth and a friend to Edd. I witnessed what they were going through. I understood their concerns. I empathized with the emotional roller coaster they were unwillingly riding. I wanted all of this to just go away as badly as they did. But I also knew that they would be the ones that would have to do the work. They would have to set the rules, light the candles and burn the incense. I couldn't move into their home with them and take over this job. The ball was now in their court.

Chapter Six:
Experiments and Data and Research, Oh My!

I had a pile of work to accomplish and only two days to get it all done. Not only was I working the Dunnam case, I was working full time and raising my son, Kyle. I had written my first book and was trying to get it published. And I was starting a ghost tour to help defray some of the costs of our research and maintenance of two cemeteries we had "adopted" to restore and preserve. I had a full plate to say the least. I felt like I hadn't slept in nearly a year. I had no social life to speak of, but I was happy.

I have to do the shameless plug at this point to explain why I began the "Haunts of the World's Most Famous Beach" ghost tours. I have to thank Karen Harvey, fellow author and ghost tour operator along with all of my friends, for giving me the nudge to begin this project. The ghost tour was pretty easy to begin since I had completed the historical research of the area and the group had helped complete documentation of the individual stories. I sold copies of the stories after the tours to help with some of the costs. I advertised and sold T-shirts. I've been told you can't have a business in Daytona Beach without having a T-shirt to sell. I wrote tour scripts and practiced them often. I walked out the tour route to establish the best stopping points and the time each stop would take. I set Jan. 10 as the date to have the first tour, with my friends serving as guinea pigs. My hope was the tours would eventually do well enough to provide all the funds needed for the cemetery restoration and preservation projects. Fortunately, this became the case. In the beginning I used some tour proceeds to help with the research costs, but those expenses eventually become nominal. Also, we get donations specifically for our research. The two cemeteries we adopted, Gethsemane Cemetery and Saints and Sinners Cemetery, are my way of giving back to the community and to help preserve some of our history. But enough about the tours, back to the case at hand.

I first emailed Dave Juliano to update him on the case. After the film was developed, I was carefully going over the photos and correlating them with the data I had collected the night of Dec. 23. There were only two positive photographic results, both taken in the backyard. The first was taken in the same location that our upside-down rainbow had been photographed. The second was taken in the area directly behind the garage. Both of these areas would never disappoint us photographically in the future.

I then turned my attention to Emily's toy bee. I established the activity area on my kitchen counter, covered it with black paper sprinkled with flour. I marked out the five-inch distance the bee had traveled, turned on a tape recorder and began to push the toy bee across the countertop slowly, counting every click it made. I noticed on occasion it would click two or even three times with just one roll. I became to realize I may have found the culprit of the clicking sounds on the tape. But no matter what evidence I had, it would still only be a purported activity as no one saw the toy actually move on that night.

After what seemed like an eternity, I finally said aloud, "one hundred and ninety five!" That was the exact number of clicks I'd heard on both tapes from our first overnighter. I looked down at the flour and realized that the same impression had been made. The bee had traveled back and forth in the flour four and a third times and left a deep impression in the center of the flour. I hit the rewind button on the tape recorder and wrote down my findings. I listened carefully to the new recording for the sound. Was the click the same as what we had recorded at the Dunnam home? Would it have the same pitch and tone to it? Did the click last for the same amount of time on tape? Would there be a difference because of recorder placement and the bee now traveling across a tile countertop instead of carpet? And would there be the 195 clicks I had just carefully counted off? Although the sound was clearer and a bit louder, it seemed to be an exact match. I attributed the clearness to the closer proximity of the recorder to the toy bee and the greater volume to my tile countertop. There was no carpet to absorb the sound. The tone and pitch were the same and all 195 clicks were there. I now fed this recording into my computer along with the sound of a click recorded at the Dunnam home and compared the two. This may seem quite silly to some, but this is one of the ways we experiment to find out the truth, or at least some form of the truth, in a case. Believe me, I don't find this tedious kind of experimentation fun at all. But it is necessary. The computer audio program showed both click sounds were an exact match, with the exception of the volume. I felt I finally had one answer of the many questions from the Dunnam house.

I continued pouring over everyone's notes, trying to find some reason this house was so active. The more data I reviewed, the less sense it all made. I returned to my library and the Internet to see if I could find any cases with activity resembling what we'd documented in the Dunnam home. It wasn't a great way to spend Christmas Eve, but it was a job that needed to be done if we were going to help this family get some peace in their own home. I hoped the Dunnam family Christmas Eve was calm, peaceful and happy. As I noted earlier, paranormal activity tends to increase during holidays and other important dates.

I spent the rest of the night researching cases on the Internet and my library, making notes and completing preparations for Christmas Day. I hadn't found any reliable cases resembling those at the Dunnam house and my spirits sank pretty low. I felt I had no one to counsel on this case, and I knew in my heart somehow time was running out for this family's safety.

Christmas morning dawned bright and warm. Kyle ripped through his gifts in record time as usual. I was pleased to see Santa had granted my "good girl" request and had left me a new digital video camera under the Christmas tree. My son and I spent the day with my family, catching up on all the usual and unusual goings on of our family. Several family members from up north called with their holiday tidings and of course, we all had to brag about how beautiful the Christmas weather was in Florida. We opened our presents and sat down for our family meal. It was over fairly painlessly in about four hours. Kyle and I thanked everyone for their gifts, gave out our hugs and kisses and returned home for what we thought would be a relaxing quiet evening together at our own home.

About twenty minutes after we arrived home, the phone rang. We hadn't even completed putting all our new booty away. Kyle hadn't had time to even get batteries into all of his new electronic games.

"Hello?" I answered as the phone rang a third time.

"Hey kiddo! Merry Christmas!" It was Edd's happy voice on the other end of the line.

"Hey Edd," I answered. "Merry Christmas. Did Santa bring you anything good this year?"

"Geesh," he exclaimed. "Beth's Mom and Dad got the family a huge telescope. This thing looks like it was built by NASA. Haven't tested it out yet, but boy a.m. I ready to. How 'bout you? Were you a good girl or a bad girl this year?"

"I haven't had enough time to be bad Edd. So, yeah, I got some cool stuff this year. How's things at the house? Anything new?" I asked.

"You mean besides the usual noises, voices and stuff moving around?" he replied. "Well, yeah. You know that Beth's Mom and Dad didn't believe us about what's going on here?"

"Yes, Beth had mentioned that to me."

"Well, it seems they are changing their minds after spending a few nights here with us," he said, laughing. "I guess being woken up a few times by knocking sounds, voices and having their blankets pulled off of them, made them firm believers that something unusual may be going on here. I actually sighed with relief when we discussed it at dinner last night. Someone, besides you, that has seen some of it, and now believes us. A real relief kiddo, a *real* relief!"

"I'm sure it was for both you and Beth," I commented. "Has the activity settled down at all? Did Beth remember to pick up the candles and incense?"

"Yeah," he said. "She got the stuff that same night after you left; been burning that smelly shit every night before we go to bed. I'll tell ya what though; it seems to be helping some. So I'll put up with the stink." He laughed loudly into the phone. "She's been taking care of the video and audio recorders too."

"Just so you know," he added. "There was one other odd thing I figured I should tell you about."

"Oh, what's that?" I asked.

"Well, I tried calling you four times before I got through. The first time the operator said, "The number you have reached is no longer in service." The second time it rang and rang and rang. I waited to see if your machine picked up, but after the 23 rings I finally hung up. The third time the operator said, "The number you have reached has been disconnected, no further information is available." Then finally on the fourth try it was dead! No ringing, no busy signal, no operator…nothing. It was the strangest thing. So I came over here to the neighbors' house and I finally got through. It was just weird."

"Do me a favor," I asked, "and call the phone company tomorrow and have your lines checked for trouble. I'll do the same. Let's rule out holiday phone traffic or technical problems before we blame it on the ghosts." I laughed.

"Sure thing kid; I just figured you'd want to know," he replied.

"Of course I want to know. I'm glad you told me. Let me know what the phone company says about your line as soon as you know.

Are you still ready for us to invade your home again tomorrow?"

"Ha! You're not invading," he said. "We enjoy your gang being here. It helps us to understand and more importantly, it helps us get a good night's sleep! Do you need us to pick anything up at the store before you get here?"

"Nah. We'll be fine. You know us Edd, always prepared," I answered.

"Okay then, we'll see you guys tomorrow; about the same time?"

"Yeah. Tell Beth I said, "Merry Christmas" and we'll see you tomorrow Edd."

I hung up the phone, wrote down notes from the conversation before heading for the shower. Before I went to bed I listened to the tape I had made of the vertical blind movements in the family room. I was really hoping the sounds would match what we had gotten on the audio portion of the video tape from our first overnighter; not so much the clicking sounds as the popping sounds. I felt sure the click sounds were related to Emily's toy bee. I listened to the tape then played the video, paying close attention to its audio. The task took several hours to complete and the worst part of it was it seemed none of the sounds from the audio matched the sounds on the audio portion of the video tape. I fed the sounds into my computer as I had done with the click sounds and realized quickly my ears had not deceived me. The sounds were from two different sources: the frequencies were completely different. My luck with the toy bee sounds was not to hold for the pop sounds. Although I had ruled out the vertical blinds as a possible culprit for the sounds, I still hadn't answered the question "What made the pop noise on the audio portion of the video tape?"

I settled into bed knowing I would have another busy day ahead of me working all day before preparing and packing our equipment. We wouldn't spend the night, but would stay at late as we could, depending on the amount and level of activity. Ros, George and I were the only ones available to go to Edd and Beth's house on Dec. 26. Everyone else was out of town visiting their relatives for the holidays. This was fine with me. From the way Edd's last email and phone call sounded, the activity seemed to have slowed a bit. I found this to be a bit unusual since I knew activity increases at significant dates. I know I am repeating myself with the "increased activity around the holidays" statement, but I can't stress this fact enough. No one is quite sure why. We can only guess that it is the remaining conscience of the once living that still wants to be a part of the holiday spirit, no pun intended.

We arrived just before 8:00 p.m. and began unpacking the equipment. Edd met us at the car and helped George carry in the equipment cases. Ros and I sat down to talk with Beth about any new happenings. She briefed us on their holidays and the time she spent with her parents. She said she ran the video tapes, but not the audio. There were so many people in the house she felt I may not be able to decipher the living from the no longer living. I assured her that her judgment was correct. She gave me three video tapes and told me she hadn't watched any of the footage. I explained she didn't need to watch the tapes; that was my job.

Edd and George stood in the kitchen talking when Emily came running into the living room. She jumped up into Beth's lap giggling. A puppy appeared from the darkened hallway. He was about 10 pounds, white with brown spots and looked to be a bulldog mixed breed. He was full of energy as he chased down his toddler prey.

"And who is this?" I asked.

"That's Little Eddy," Edd said from the kitchen.

"Did Santa leave him under your tree too Edd?" I asked with a laugh.

"Yup, he's a handful" Edd said. "But the kids have fun with him." Edd retrieved the puppy and took him out the front door to do "his business."

"Boy oh boy Beth, you sure have your hands full," I said, turning to her.

"Yeah, but I enjoy it," she said. "I'm going to go get Emily ready for bed. I'll be back in a little bit."

"Sure Beth," I replied. "We'll go out back and see if anything is going on out there."

Ros and I grabbed some equipment just as Edd returned with the puppy.

"Hey, let me grab my jacket and I'll head out with you," he said.

"Okay Edd, we'll wait for you," I answered.

It was a little chilly outside, 62 degrees. The wind was calm and the humidity was low, only 46 percent. I took some pictures with both cameras as Ros took temperature readings and George worked the EMF. Edd stood near me talking about things going on in the house. As he spoke, the colder the temperature became. Ros found that the area temperature was 62 degrees but the air directly around Edd and I was 32 degrees. As Edd and I moved, the coldness followed. If Edd stopped talking about the household's activities, the air around us would warm to the ambient air temperature. If he began talking about the activity again, the air temperature around he and I would drop quickly to 32 degrees again. We kept taking readings for a little over an hour as Edd stopped and started talking. It was the strangest thing. "Okay, I'm not giving you ghosties the spotlight anymore," he said as he made a zipping motion over his lips.

We headed back into the house and as Beth opened the door she asked Edd, "Did you shut the TV off?"

"Nope, must be the ghosties again!" Edd replied with a bellowing laugh.

"Has this been happening more lately Beth?" I asked.

"Yeah," she answered. "It has been getting so much worse and we had the cable company out to check all the connections again. And the power company out to check for whatever it is they check for. And my parents even bought us another new TV. But it just keeps shutting off."

"And sometimes turning on, don't forget that Beth," Edd added.

"Oh, that's right," Beth said. "The other night Edd came to bed later than I did. I heard him shut the TV off. And after about two minutes or so, it came back on. He went back out into the living room to shut it off and before he could set the remote onto the table, it came back on again. It went on like this for about 20 minutes. He finally unplugged the whole entertainment center."

"Well, let's see if they try it tonight," I said.

Each of us grabbed a two-way radio and handheld equipment as we began setting up the video recording equipment throughout the house. We made sure there was coverage of the family room, kitchen, hallway, living room and Emily's bedroom. We set up audio recorders in the small bedroom, garage and in Edd and Beth's bedroom. George taped down all the cords and wires so we wouldn't trip over them in the darkness. Ros double-checked the viewing angles. As I sat on the couch talking with Edd about how he and Beth were holding up Little Eddy came lumbering into the room. He flopped down in the center of the area rug and fell asleep.

Edd explained having Beth's family around was good and bad.

"It was nice to have other witnesses, but they wanted to explain everything away," he said. "You know, it was the wind from an open window, their imagination, they were dreaming, the usual; even when the new telescope they bought us began to spin around by itself and Emily's toys began moving across the floor by themselves. The big one was when Emily's two floor mobiles started swinging back and forth by themselves. We all sat here and watched it, even the cats. The lights, sounds and movement, it was a hoot." He continued, "The one I thought had them totally convinced was when their blankets kept being taken off of them at night, even when they were awake. Hell! The ghosties haven't even done that to Beth and me yet. But something kept them from solidly believing. And then, of course they gave me the speech on fearing for Beth and Emily's safety."

"Did they really feel that you would let Beth or Emily be harmed on purpose Edd?" I asked. "No. I just think they wanted to spend more time with them and offered to have them go up to Maryland until I could get this mess settled," he said.

"I see," I commented.

I looked down at the puppy sleeping soundly on the floor and noticed his tail beginning to wag. He rolled over onto his back and his back leg began kicking, the way it would if someone found his tickle spot. The EMF was sitting silently next to me on the couch began showing a 3. I glanced at it then back to the puppy.

Just then Edd said, "Dusty? Do you see that?"

"Um, yeah Edd, I see it," I answered.

I called to George and Ros on the radio. "I need both of you in the living room now. Come quickly and quietly!"

They both quietly walked into the living room from different directions. I motioned for them to look at the puppy and Ros's mouth dropped open.

"Can you see it?" I asked quietly.

"Yes! Oh my God," Ros said.

"Holy shit! Am I seeing what I think I'm seeing?" George asked. "Yes!"

We were all seeing it. There was an unseen hand tickling the puppy's belly. We could clearly see the indent of fingers rubbing up and down, and side to side on the soft underbelly of the small dog obviously enjoying his unseen friend. His leg continued to kick into the air at nothing as we all watched in amazement for nearly 15 minutes. The EMF continued to whine at a steady 3, but there were no temperature variations. Just as suddenly as the petting began, it ceased. Little Eddy rolled over with a look of confusion on his face as if to say 'why did you guys stop rubbing my belly?' He dragged himself off the rug and headed to the kitchen for a snack and a drink. I had a feeling it would be another long night for us in the Dunnam house.

It suddenly felt very warm in the house, so I decided to step outside to get some fresh air and try to wrap my logical mind around what I had just witnessed. I grabbed my cameras and stated my intentions of checking out the backyard again. Ros, George and Edd followed. No one said anything, but I think a few minutes out of the house was what we all needed at that moment.

We made our way to the backyard and stood directly behind the family room. No one said a word. Everyone was taking readings, jotting notes, and trying to deal with the paranormal experience we just had in our own ways. George, to this day, will still not speak of that experience. Edd just stood there with his hands in his pockets staring at the house he once thought would be a happy home for his family. I could see the stress, anger, confusion and disgust on his face.

Just then he looked up and said, "Hey, Dusty, do you guys see that?" as he pointed towards the roof between the family room and the master bedroom.

"See what Edd?" we replied.

"The mist; there's a huge mist over the house and it's moving this way," he answered.

Edd began walking towards the area where he said he saw the mist as I began snapping photos, my mind in disbelief that he was actually seeing this. Boy, would I be wrong! I snapped the first picture, and sure enough, Edd was pointing directly at a mist moving across the back of his home. A chill ran up my spine, goose bumps rose on my arms and I suddenly realized that this man could see these paranormal anomalies with his own eyes. At first I thought it was a wonderful gift, and then realized what a great burden this gift could become for someone. Imagine seeing things that no one else could or would and having to stay quiet when you did see them, never knowing if what you were seeing was a living person or one who had passed on. And what if this gift was hereditary? Could he have passed it onto Emily or the new baby? We would soon find out.

We heard Little Eddy begin to bark from inside the family room. We returned inside and see if he was all right and to check on the equipment. I commented his loud bark would probably scare the crap out of me when I viewed the video tapes from the family room. Everyone else laughed as we headed inside.

Just as we stepped through the front door, Beth appeared from the hallway. "Edd, can you please take him outside, he'll wake up Emily with that barking" she said.

"Sure thing Momma," Edd said as he snatched up Little Eddy and headed out the door once again.

We made our usual rounds to check equipment and log anything worth noting. Emily slept soundly. Beth finished her nightly chores and was getting ready for bed. The cats were snoozing in their chosen spots and we started to prepare for the long night ahead of us. Edd came back into the house followed closely by the puppy, which eased himself up onto the couch and curled up to go to sleep.

Edd and Beth said their good-nights and headed off to their bedroom. We set up camp in the living room and turned the television's volume down. George and I discussed the possibility of electrical problems as a source for the TV turning itself off, but agreed they were nothing more than theories. Ros watched the silent TV screen and wrote notes.

Around 1:30 a.m., the 'fun' began. It began with the noises we had come to expect from this house: knocking, banging, the heavy dragging noise. And there was the new one Ros and George hadn't heard yet, the sound like a horse was galloping across the roof. It was so loud I couldn't imagine how anyone could sleep through it. Back and forth, back and forth. Heavy and loud, it continued for 13 minutes. Ros stayed inside with the audio recorders microphone held as close to the ceiling as she could get it, while George and I went into the yard to see if we could see anything on the roof. Nothing was visible as I began to take photos and George took EMF and temperature readings.

This large mist with orbs was also photographed
during the loud sounds on the roof.

After the photos showed no additional activity and the galloping
sounds died down, we tried to settle back in for the rest of the night.
We went back to filling in our log sheets and jotting notes and
impressions of what we just experienced. After everyone had time to
finish their note-taking, we discussed the loud galloping sounds. We
had experienced a lot of firsts at the Dunnam home and this was just
another to add to that growing list. We began forming theories for the
loud sounds. Could it be raccoons or opossums in the attic? Could the
noise be coming from some problem with the heating ducts?

As we talked, the telescope began to spin around on its own. Ros
said jokingly, "Well, I guess no matter what theories we come up

with, whatever is here is going to let us know we're wrong."

"It would seem that way," I replied.

The telescope turned from side to side, and then in and up and down motion as we watched in disbelief. It moved slowly, but fast enough to see it with the naked eye. I thought of the scene from *Poltergeist* when the researcher tells the homeowner about taking several hours to capture an event on film, adding "this wouldn't register with the naked eye." The homeowner opens the door to show the researcher a room filled with visible activity. The telescope didn't have enough clearance next to the wall to do a complete 360 degree turn, but as much as it did move, it never hit into the wall. I took several still photographs especially a very interesting one. Not only did it show an orb and mist activity in the hallway emerging from the attic crawl space entrance in the direction of the telescope, but also it seemed to show the cat looking in the direction of the activity. The photograph also showed a line of mist between the bathroom to Emily's bedroom. This would later prove to be a huge piece of evidence in the case. One real frustration was despite all our carefully positioned video camera angles, one spot not filmed was in the direction of the telescope.

The activities finally began to settle down around 4:30 a.m. By the time the sun arose we were wasted: tired, hungry and drained from the constant energy that kept us up all night; so much for our plans not to spend the night at the Dunnam house. Even the cats and the puppy seemed to have had a rough night with little sleep.

We broke down the equipment; made sure everything was labeled correctly, cleaned up our mess and packed the car. I wasn't looking forward to the drive home and unpacking. George and I both had to work in just a few hours. But it was well worth the sacrifice of personal time to have had such an active night. We had some great evidence and superb experiences from the night at the Dunnam house.

It is best to have at least two people witness activity, but on this night, we had three and even four or five witnesses. I looked forward to viewing our evidence, but realized with all the video and audio we had, it may take a week to go through it all. I also had to view the three six-hour-long video tapes Beth made for us. But it would all have to wait until I had some badly needed sleep, a desperately needed shower, and a good hot meal.

Chapter Seven:
The Madness Continues

I got to bed around 7:30 a.m. Luckily, my boss left an email stating he didn't have any work for me that day and giving me the day off with pay. What a relief! I could sleep as long as I wanted and not worry about getting up for work. But as is often my luck, things never seem to work out the way I plan them, especially when it comes to sleep. The phone rang at 12:15 p.m. It was Edd on the other end of the line.

"Hey kiddo, did I wake you?" he said.

"Edd?" I said sleepily. "Um, no, well, yes, but it's okay. What's up?"

"I just got in from work and Beth wanted me to let you know what happened this morning after you guys left."

"Okay, what happened?"

"I just have to laugh about it now, but it wasn't so funny this morning. First of all, me and Beth slept really well last night, and we both wanted to thank you guys for that. I slept so well in fact I slept through the alarm and was late for work. Well, with what happened I would have been late for work anyhow."

"Okay Edd, I'm glad you both slept well, but, get to the point please, I'm running on very little sleep and may conk out on you if you don't," I replied.

"Oh, yeah, right. Well, Emily started crying this morning wanting her diaper changed and her morning bottle. So Beth got up and had to go take a piss. You know, being pregnant and all, her bladder comes first." He laughed and continued. "She went to get into the bathroom in our bedroom, and the door wouldn't open. The knob turned fine, and the door actually opened about a quarter of an inch, but that was it. She tried to push against it and still couldn't get in. She finally wound up peeing her pants. She yelled at me to get up and take care of Emily while she cleaned herself up."

"Damn Edd! Is Beth all right?" I asked, alarmed.

"Hell yeah, she's fine; more embarrassed than anything," he continued. "Beth was in the front bathroom cleaning herself up and I took care of Emme's diaper and bottle situation. Then I tried the bathroom door myself. Shit Dusty, even I couldn't open that son of a bitch!"

"Did you figure out why Edd?"

"Yep! I went outside and jimmied the window and climbed in. You're not going to believe this shit, but someone, or something took the rubber-backed bathroom rug and shoved it up against the back of the bathroom door. It was wedged in under the door so tight that it took me several tries to pull that sucker loose. "

"Okay Edd, give me a second here. There is only the one door leading into or out of that bathroom, right?"

"Right!"

"And the bathroom window was locked form the inside, right?"

"Right!"

"And there was no one inside the bathroom when you climbed in through the window, right?"

"Right!"

"And the only people in the house were you, Beth and Emily,

right?"

"Right again kiddo!"

"So what do you and Beth think happened Edd?" I asked.

"Well, as for me, I can't figure out any way the rug could have gotten jammed in like that. You know, 'cause the door opens in and the rug was jammed in like someone did it from the inside. But no one was inside. And Beth, she is now thinking that the ghosties are trying to hurt her or cause a problem with the pregnancy. I'm thinking that maybe her Mom's mini speeches may have something to do with that line of thinking though. To be quite honest Dusty, I have no clue how or why it happened, only that it did."

"Well Edd, I appreciate you calling to let me know about this," I said quietly. "If it makes Beth feel any better, maybe you could temporarily take that door off the hinges and just leave it open, at least until after the new baby arrives."

"One more thing Dusty," he added. "I don't want to forget to tell you, the phone company was here this morning and said there is nothing wrong with our phone lines or phones. But just now when I tried to call you, the same shit happened again."

"You weren't able to get through?"

"Nope it took three tries. I decided to just give up on using the house phone and use my cell phone, but even it wouldn't work from inside the house. I decided to call you from the front yard, same as last time too. First it said the number was no longer in service, then out of order, and then that long silence. It's weird, it's like they don't want me to talk to you. And I had just finished talking on the house phone with a client and on my cell phone with one of my buds," Edd said.

"That is very odd," I said. "Maybe the ghosts don't want you calling me Edd. I don't know what to tell you about the phones until the phone company comes here. I am having my lines checked tomorrow. Just keep reporting the problems to the phone company and keep me informed of when it happens, how many times it happens and how many tries it takes you to get through. And don't forget, there is always email and instant messaging. Hopefully we'll figure something out with this shit."

"I hope so Dusty, Beth is starting to get scared," he said. "I've never seen her like this before. And I feel so helpless. I can take on anything and come out on top, but this shit is too much. I need to protect my family and at the same time, I can't."

I could hear the desperation and despair in his voice. A macho, tough guy like Edd, who couldn't fight off the victimizer of his family, was experiencing the biggest blow his ego would probably ever take.

"Not to mention the fact that I've lost so much work," he added. "With the holidays, prenatal doctor visits, and ghosts keeping me up all night, I'll be lucky to make our bills this month. I think I'll pay the rent last." Edd laughed loudly. "It would serve him right to not get another dime out of us. I even asked him if there was something here we should be afraid of or that might harm Beth or the kids and the son of a bitch said, 'No.' Now I know why he moved out in the middle of the night and won't step foot back into this house."

I could see how the sleepless nights and stress were beginning to wear on Edd and most likely the rest of the Dunnam family. I let him vent and rant for several minutes before I interrupted to say "Edd, if it comes down to it, let the landlord take you to court for any money you wind up owing him." I continued. "I'll go into court with the evidence we've collected and let the judge know my feelings on how this guy lied to you and placed your family in direct danger. It's also time to look as this whole thing more seriously than you have before. Do you want to try to cleanse the house and stay living there? Or do you want to try to move and start over in another location? I know it's been kind of fun for you up until this point, but the fun is now over. What do you want to do?"

"Let me talk it over with Beth," he answered. "I know we can't afford to move. Hell, we've only been here for 10 months. We were just starting to get ahead when this stuff got really bad and I started missing work. And the added expense of a new baby coming doesn't help right now either. Not that I don't want the little guy, but the ghosties I could have done without. And Beth is in no shape to be packing our home or moving until after the baby comes. Shit Dusty, I don't know what to do."

"Well, talk it over with Beth and let me know what you both decide" I said. "You know I'll be behind you 100 percent, whatever you decide Edd."

"Thanks kiddo. I really don't know how we could have gotten through this shit without you," Edd said.

"Awe, come on Edd, you'll make me blush or something," I said as humbly as I could. "Don't sweat it, that's what I'm here for."

"All right then, I'll let you get back to sleep," he said. "I'll call or email if anything else happens, okay?"

"Sure thing Edd," I replied. "Tell Beth I said 'Hi.'"

"I will. Talk to you soon." And with that Edd hung up the phone.

I wanted to go right back to sleep, but with this new information, my mind again began to race. I kept picturing the master bath in my mind to try to come up with some rational explanation as to how the rug could have moved as it did. And now it was my turn to feel the desperation and despair. No matter what I now said to Edd and Beth, it never seemed to be right or enough to ease their fears. I felt like I wasn't giving them any answers and was only being patronizing. I was really trying to help, but felt as though no matter what I said or did, it was not going to be enough until the activity stopped altogether or they moved out of the home.

I slept restlessly, and when I woke up at 3:30 p.m. I was in a really bad mood. Even coffee didn't help. I couldn't stop thinking about the master bathroom at the Dunnam house. I drew a map and went into my own bathroom to see if it were possible to recreate the incident from outside. It was not. The only way I could recreate the scene was to attach a piece of fishing line to the rug and pull it through from the outside. The rug sort of wedged under the door, but not enough to prevent me from forcing the door open. With just a couple of good shoves I could easily get through the doorway. This was an awful lot of trouble to go through just to make someone pee in his or her pants, so I couldn't imagine Edd or Beth pulling a hoax like this. I had no trouble setting up the scene from the inside, but then I had no way out. This was frustrating, but then there were many frustrating things about this case.

The phone rang and it was Suzi with some interesting news. She had discussed some of the aspects of the Dunnam case with the owner of the video production company located next to her office. Since Edd and Beth had both waived their confidentiality rights, I really didn't have a problem with the team discussing the case with others, especially if someone might come up with solutions we hadn't considered. Suzi said the producer was very interested in the story and asked for my telephone number to discuss doing a documentary about the case. I told Suzi I would have to speak with Edd and Beth about it first. If they were up for it, I'd let her know. This might be a temporary solution to some of the Dunnam's money trouble. I'd heard some production companies pay quite well for material or use of a location.

I first called Troy Taylor, founder and president of the American Ghost Society, my mentor. I asked for his thoughts on this project, and he told me to read the fine print and to keep my eyes wide open. When he had agreed to film *The St. Francisville Experiment*, the producers had not informed him that if they did not get any paranormal activity on film, they would insert their own. When Troy saw the finished product, he was so angry at the results he sued the production company. Troy said the production was akin to "Blair Witch Meets House on Haunted Hill." Such productions can haunt your reputation as a serious researcher, no pun intended. I thanked Troy for his guidance and advice and hung up the phone.

My next call was to the Dunnam household and I received a busy signal. Assuming Beth was online, I signed onto AOL to look for her or Edd. They weren't online. I tried calling again and got a recording stating the number was no longer in service. The first thought that popped into my head was that, their money problems are worse than I thought. Perhaps they were unable to pay their phone bill. But then I thought, what if the "ghosties" really didn't want me to contact Edd and Beth? Could Edd have been right about this? I tried one more time and got silence on the line. I agreed with Edd, it was eerie. I called Edd's cell phone and finally got through. We tried to hold our conversation, but his phone kept fading and there was a lot of static over the line. I managed to tell him to get onto his computer and I would chat with him in instant message. He agreed and hung up.

Nearly 20 minutes passed before I finally saw Edd's screen name pop up. He explained he had trouble getting signed on. "Must be the ghosties again," he typed. I explained Suzi's encounter and asked if he and Beth were interested in doing a documentary. I wrote their lives would no longer be private if they agreed to do this project. Emily would grow up as the kid who lived in the "scary ghost house." These were things he and Beth needed to consider before saying, yes. Edd replied Beth was sitting at the computer with him and they were discussing the offer as we typed. They decided they could both handle the publicity. As for Emily, well, it might net them enough money to pay for any therapy she may need in the future. The boys, on the other hand, would just have to deal with the fact they were part time residents of the scary ghost house. He added a "LOL," chat abbreviation for laughing out loud.

I warned them of the problems this venture might bring them, adding it is not my place to make decisions for any client. I consider it my job to keep clients informed of any evidence and publicity. They both agreed to do the project if it proved somehow beneficial to them and made my research group look as professional as we had always been with them on this case. I agreed if the producer wanted to turn this project into some form of *Blair Witch Project*, we would all run, not walk, away. I told them I would set up a time on the 30th to stop by so they could meet the producer. They agreed on 4:00 p.m. time.

I phoned the producer Vickie, and spoke with her for nearly an hour to try to feel her out and see the direction she wanted to take with this project. I explained if it were to be anything other than a documentary, she could forget the whole thing. She agreed to keep it in the documentary format and added she wanted to bring a couple of actors and her cameraman on the 30th to meet Edd and Beth. I didn't see a problem with this, so I told her that would be fine. She asked if she could stop by to meet me that evening and to have me sign a release form for the project. I told her I would be in all evening and to come on by the house after work. I said good bye and went to take my shower.

Let me explain that I do my best thinking when I'm in the bathroom. I'm not joking; I'm deadly serious about this. Vickie seemed to be genuinely interested in the documentary but something was nagging me about her. I couldn't quite put my finger on it. I'm generally a good judge of people and can usually tell if they are trying to pull the wool over my eyes. With the Dunnam's privacy and my reputation about to be on the line, I had my eyes as wide open as I could get them.

Vickie finally arrived at 5:15 p.m. At first I was impressed with her professionalism. She had a binder prepared with the company logo, business cards and release forms. She also had a four-page outline for the "screenplay." We discussed the Dunnam case for nearly an hour. As she was heading out my front door, she suddenly stopped and said, "Have a look at what I've written. If you see anything that needs to be changed, feel free to edit away." That should have been my first clue Vickie was up to something. I still wasn't quite sure what it was, so I shook her hand and told her I'd look it over that evening.

After I ate dinner, I sat down at the computer to check emails, and the first one I came to was from Vickie. It was a copy of the outline for the project, and another copy of the release form. I opened the file and was horrified to see plans for a *Blair Witch Project* production. It began innocently enough, but then the actors were sucked back into the house at dawn, never to be heard from again! I typed throughout the night and well into the early morning. Before I knew it, I'd written an entire screenplay. I sent a copy of it to the Screenwriter's Guild, registering it as mine. Later I would thank my lucky starts I did. I also sent a copy to my publisher, and a close friend, just in case I needed verification I had written it.

The following morning Vickie phoned early.

"Hiya Dusty," she said. "Did you have a chance to see what I wrote?"

"Hey Vickie," I answered. "Yes, I did. I rewrote the whole thing last night."

"Oh? Great," she replied. "I knew it needed some work and your expertise."

"I'm no expert Vickie. There are no experts in this field, only people with more experience than others."

"Well, whatever," she said. "As long as you have something for us to work from, that's great. If you don't mind, I'll stop over in about an hour and pick up a copy to see how you did."

I suddenly felt like Bugs Bunny when he turns into a giant lollipop with the word "sucker" printed across it. This producer had just got me to write her screenplay for her without asking or paying me to do so. I was so mad at myself for allowing myself to be used in that way, but then I thought "What the heck, if it helps Edd and Beth to get a nice chunk of change, so be it."

I spent the next two days going through reports, log sheets, event maps, listening to audio recordings and watching video footage from the Dunnam house. It was becoming very obvious that not only was the activity increasing in frequency, but in intensity as well. All of the activity still seemed, for whatever reason, to be centered near the hallway bookcase and Emily's room. There was still a good deal of activity in other rooms of the house, but the most intense activity was in these two locations. Emily's room still had no echo in it. The dead air in that room was frightening. The cold spots in her room were more frequent and the level of temperature drop was greater than in the past two months. What had begun as an eight to 10 degree difference was now ranging from 18 to 29 degrees. The cold spot did move inside the room, but in a very limited area. It was always detected in front of Emily's closet door and it would move into the center of the room then back towards the closet door again.

While going through all of this data, I noticed something intriguing about the audio portion of the video tapes. Sounds we clearly heard while filming were not present on the tapes. The sound of Little Eddy barking in the family room while we were outside wasn't on the video tape recorded at the time. There was also a tape recorded in Emily's room that didn't capture her crying. Her crying was on the audio tape, but not on the audio portion of the video tape shot at the same exact time. Was it possible for the entities, spirits or ghosts to manipulate sound? How could they prevent certain noises from recording on our tapes? Why would they not want us to hear these noises and sounds? Did I really want to know the answer to that last question? Things were getting freakier.

The hallway and bookcase were another frustration. I don't get spooked easily, but walking down that hallway at night, even with lights on and someone with me, creeped me out something terrible. It was like you could feel people standing in the hallway, watching you, who didn't like the fact you were in their space. The Dunnam case resulted in our No. 1 equipment rule: always bring a spare change of underwear. Always. The voices, footsteps, knockings, cold spots, hot spots and visible apparitions in the hallway had become not just daily, but almost hourly events. I suspected the upside-down rainbow we saw over the roof was somehow linked to the bookcase, but how? I hoped Kelly Weaver would soon shed some light on this case.

The family room still had plenty of noise emanating from it, but now the bangings, knockings and dragging noises could be heard during both daytime and nighttime hours. The electrical problems in the house were getting worse as well. Light bulbs lasted three to eight hours now. The brand new TV turned on and off every few minutes. It became so frustrating for Beth she finally just started watching the TV in the bedroom. Until one night, when she and Edd were having sex in their bedroom, the TV kept turning on and off as it had done before. Unfortunately, Edd was not very interested in the TV and wanted to finish what he had started. But poor Beth later told me that she felt as if someone was watching her from inside the TV set every time it would turn on.

She said, "It was very upsetting and unnerving."

She swore she could see faces looking out at them that night.

I know how upset some of the experiences I had in that house made me, but I could leave at anytime. Beth was stuck there. She didn't work, so even Edd had some time away from the madness. Plus she was dealing with a toddler and she was pregnant. I noticed their personalities had begun to change even more since I had first met them. They were no longer the happy-go-lucky couple that liked to relax on the couch together, cuddling and watching TV while sipping a glass of wine. They now sat on different pieces of furniture, went through a good deal of wine and beer almost every night, and rarely had a kind word for one another anymore.

I hate to say it, but a haunting, especially when a negative energy involved, can tear a family apart. That is exactly what was happening inside the walls of the Dunnam house. Edd's boys spent less and less time with their Dad. Emily spent more and more time alone in her room watching videos on her television set and holding conversations with unseen people. Edd and Beth were beginning to grow apart emotionally and physically. It was hard to watch, so I spoke with them about my observations as often as I could, and tried to reassure them that they would get their lives back eventually. Not much comfort, I know, but what else could I do at that time? I still had no solid answers and they were still coming to terms with the fact that this was not fun anymore.

The 30th finally arrived and Vickie, her cameraman and three actors were standing at my front door, right on time. Introductions were made all around, and I remarked to Kevin how much he looked like Charlie Sheen.

He laughed and said, "I guess that's a good thing since I'm his stunt double."

"Oh wow! That's must be an interesting job," I said.

"It can be" he replied.

Vickie passed out binders to everyone that hadn't all ready gotten one. She handed me a new copy of the script and the first thing I noticed was it had her name as the author. I flipped through the script and noticed it was the exact screenplay I had written only two nights ago. I bit my tongue until I could get her alone to discuss her name on my work.

We gathered up our belongings and headed out for the vehicles. Just then Ros started going nuts looking for her car keys.

"They were right here on the table by you Vickie," Ros asked. "Did you pick them up by mistake?"

"Nope," Vickie replied. "I only have my own car keys."

We helped Ros search for her keys for as long as we could but soon realized if we didn't head out, we would be late for our meeting with Edd and Beth. Normally they wouldn't have minded if we were running late, but the boys would be coming over in a couple of hours. Edd didn't like discussing the house's problems in front of them anymore than was absolutely necessary. I told Ros to ride with me and we would find her keys when we got back to the house.

We looked like some bizarre convoy heading down Interstate 4: Kevin and his girlfriend Jennifer in his *Mustang*, Vickie in her brand new Saturn, the cameraman in his *Econoline* van, two actresses in a red *Iroc* with T-tops, and Ros and I leading the pack in my little granny car, a Buick *Regal*. When we arrived at their house, Edd and the puppy were in the front yard playing with Emily. It was odd to be there during daylight hours and to see the family enjoying their day. If I didn't know what was going on behind that door, I would have thought they were a normal, happy family, living an ordinary life in a normal house like everyone else on the street.

Edd greeted Ros and I in his usual manner with a big tight hug, and I introduced him to the film crew. He invited us in, offering everyone drinks, snacks and a seat. Vickie began discussing the film project with Edd and Beth as Ros and I showed the rest of the group around, pointing out where certain events had taken place. When we went back into the living room, I noticed that Beth had an odd look on her face. I motioned for her to meet me in the kitchen and she did.

"Is something wrong Beth?" I asked.

"Yeah, Vickie doesn't want to give us any money," she said, "not for the story, for acting in the film, not even for letting them stay in our home for about a week. I just think that there is something wrong with that deal."

"You're right Beth. There is something *very* wrong with that. Let me have a little talk with her," I said.

When I walked back into the living room, Vickie was asking everyone to sign the release forms and wage forms. She explained all of the actors would get one half of one percent of the film's net profits, the cameraman would get 30 percent, she would get 50 percent, I would get one percent and five percent would be donated to charity as a tax write off.

I quickly asked, "Why do you get 50 percent Vickie?"

"I get 40 percent for being the producer, that's a really hard job and takes a great deal of time to do'" she said. "I also get 10 percent for writing the script."

Now I may have been born at night, but it wasn't last night. Thankfully I had done my homework on what actors, producers, writers and the rest of a production crew typically receive. So of course I chimed in with my two cents.

"Um, Vickie?" I began. "It's my understanding a producer does not get paid anything from the production of a film. A producer earns money on aftermarket items such as video and DVD sales, posters, movie promotions and things like that. Also, since I wrote the screenplay, shouldn't I be the one who is getting the 10 percent for it, not to mention the fact my name should be on it, not yours? And while we're on the subject, Edd and Beth need to get compensated for the use of their home and would be entitled to the same pay rate as the other actors if you use them in the film. Especially Edd since he has been in the movies before. And lastly, this half percent for the actors," I paused, "standard rate is five percent with someone of Kevin's standing getting 10 percent to 20 percent. It's also standard to be paid from gross, not net. If you pay these people from your net profits, you can find a myriad of ways to spend the profits as to cut down on the amount of money they would actually see. So, do you want to rethink these terms or continue with them the way they are? Or should I continue to quote SAG (Screen Actors Guild) rates to you?" I jumped down off of my soapbox and sat quietly.

Vickie sat there for a moment with a look of horror on her face. Kevin and Jennifer actually applauded me and one of the women actresses grabbed her cell phone to call her agent to get his advice on the situation. Just as she was finishing explaining how Vickie was trying to screw everyone out of his or her money, her cell phone died. She looked down at it and said, "That's funny. I just had a full charge on the battery."

Edd said loudly from the kitchen, "It's not funny in this house. In this house that is normal."

I grabbed my camera and snapped a picture of the actress just as she was speaking and was not very surprised to see a bright orb directly over her and her cell phone.

Vickie tried convincing everyone this was the way things were done. It didn't work. Everyone decided to walk away from the project right then and there. It was a huge relief for me. I didn't need the added stress and work of a project like this right now. And I really didn't think Edd and Beth did either. If the money was there, it might have been different. Since it was not, it was best to walk away and save our sanity, privacy and reputations. I realized Edd and Beth were a bit disappointed, so before I left I tried to reassure them that walking away from this project was for the best, especially since Vickie had been less than forthright from the start. Ros and I said our good byes and we left for home.

I ranted to Ros most of the way home about Vickie. Ros said she was convinced Vickie, accidentally or on purpose, had picked up her car keys. I didn't realize it at the time, but it was the first time I had left the Dunnam house without doing my protection speech: "No entities, spirits or ghosts of any kind are allowed to follow me home. You all have to stay here or move on to another plane." I also didn't cleanse the car or myself. I was too upset to be thinking straight. I would soon find out just how important this step is in doing an investigation.

After arriving home Ros asked if she could borrow my car to run a couple of errands since she still hadn't found her car keys. Sure, I told her and she headed out the door. She, George and I were planning on having dinner together later that night, so I checked my email and tried to unwind by playing some *Tetris* on Kyle's

Playstation. It was a nice cool night, so I left the front door open. The breeze coming through the screen door was nice after the long hot humid summer and warmer-than-average autumn we'd had. I was knocking out the colored blocks left and right, climbing the Tetris ladder of success as quickly as my fingers would allow me to when the phone rang. I picked it up and said, "Hello?" but there was no response. There was a weird static and then silence. I hung up the phone, sat back onto the couch when the phone rang again. Again, there was only static and then silence. I took the phone with me this time and I sat smoking a cigarette, waiting for it to ring again. I paused my game and was chomping at the bit to get back to it. I had an odd feeling it was Edd or Beth trying to call. The phone rang for a third time and sure enough it was Edd on the other end.

"Finally! I thought I'd never get through to you kiddo," he stated loudly.

"Hi Edd," I said, laughing. "I knew it was you."

"You've got to listen to this," he said. "Let me know if you can hear it or not, okay?"

"Okay, Edd. What is it I'm listening to?"

"Honestly Dusty, I don't know what it is."

"Okay Edd. Let me listen."

I muted the volume on the TV and turned the volume up on my phone. As I listened I heard a loud knocking sound coming through the phone.

"I hear it Edd. What the heck is that?"

"I don't know kiddo. I'm standing outside the family room and the boys are inside with the blinds open looking out at me. The knocking sound is coming from the windows, but we can't see anything that is making the sound. And the weirdest part is, it's moving across the windows! Back and forth and up and down, no real set pattern to it, but it's definitely moving around," Edd said. "The boys came into the living room thinking I was in the backyard hammering on something. They looked shocked when they saw me sitting there watching TV. Beth broke out a cheap tape recorder and has been taping it since before I finally got through to you. I think she took a couple of pictures too."

"That's great Edd, tell Beth "thank you" from me. Did it start at any particular time?"

"Not that we're aware of Dusty, it just started when the boys went in to finish folding their laundry and to play some *Playstation* game. Everything is status quo here, nothing out of the ordinary as far as what we're doing tonight, just a standard night."

"And you had trouble getting through on the phone, how many times did you try and on which phones Edd?" I asked.

"Three tries, twice with the house phone and the third time on the cell phone in the yard. That went through," he answered.

I was jotting notes of the conversation when suddenly there were three loud popping sounds which sounded like someone firing a large caliber handgun. It was so loud I nearly dropped the phone. Then there was a high-pitched whine on the phone line and then the same static as I had heard before. The line went dead. I tried to call Edd back and got silence the first time, the operator recording the second time and on the third, I finally got through. Edd answered the phone and said the noises had stopped after a series of loud popping sounds. His phone went dead and later when he called me back, he told me he had gone back into the house to make sure Beth and the kids were all right. I told him not to worry about calling me back; I assumed the "ghosties" were up to their old phone tricks again. I told him to call me back anytime he needed me or if the noises started up again. He agreed and we said our good-nights.

I finished my notes and went back to my *Tetris* game. I tried to keep my mind on the game so I could relax a bit, not very easy to do when with a case like the Dunnam house. I thought about going over to their house, but realized there would be little I could do if the activity had stopped. I managed to make it to a *Tetris* level I had never been to before and just as I was about to finish the level, I heard my squeaky front gate open. So did my dog. She started barking intently out the screen door. I figured it was Ros or George coming in for dinner. I turned my head to see a shadow move up to the screen door, but no one opened the door. I got a bit upset Ros or George would take their sweet time to come in because the Damned dog kept barking her head off. I paused the game and went to the door to see what the heck was going on. To my surprise, no one was at the door. I looked out and the front gate was closed securely and there were no vehicles other than mine in the driveway. I opened the screen door to let the dog out and as I did, the front porch light exploded! I don't mean it burned out; the bulb had literally exploded in its socket. There were broken bits of glass all over my front porch stoop.

My dog Drega took about two steps outside the screen door, stopped, sniffed the air and raced back into the house and ran under my bed. I smelled whatever it was, too; a foul odor I couldn't quite identify. I reached for the light switch inside the house and turned off the porch light before I went to find another light bulb. I looked towards the TV and saw the picture was messed up. There were weird rainbow lines flipping across the picture tube. I wish I could explain it better than that, but I can't. I sat, grabbed the remote and turned the TV off and on again and now the picture was gone altogether. There was just a quarter-inch wide rainbow colored line running horizontally across the picture tube.

Both the porch light and TV are on the same circuit and switches, so I thought the switch or breaker may be bad. I hoped it wasn't anything to do with the breakers because I had just paid a small fortune to redo all the wiring in the house and put in all new breakers. I reluctantly turned my game off and went to start dinner.

When George and Ros arrived, I told them about the phone and porch light. They were both concerned I had forgotten to cleanse the car and myself before leaving the Dunnam house on our last visit. They both thought this may have something to do with the phone troubles and the electrical problems. I had a spare outlet and light switch, so George changed them both out. He checked the breaker box and tested the breakers but there was nothing out of the ordinary with any of them. He even replaced the porch light bulb, teaching me how to use a raw potato to remove a broken light bulb from its socket. George is a great friend and I rely on him a great deal when I have a "honey-do" list. Sometimes it's hard being single, especially when you don't know how to fix or repair something, but George always helps out. And he always appreciates a good home cooked meal and some quiet time away from his busy life.

As we sat at the dinner table, Ros told us how she found her car keys. She said she stopped by Vickie's and made Vickie check through her purse. Ros said when she first asked politely, Vickie refused. After two more polite requests, Ros said she told Vickie, in no longer polite terms, she needed to check her purse for the car keys, otherwise Ros would not only do bodily harm to Vickie then look for the keys herself, but she would haunt Vickie's every waking moment for the rest of her days. The thought of sweet passive Ros taking out all of her frustrations on Vickie was very appealing to me. Vickie finally opened her purse and within three seconds discovered Ros's car keys sitting right on top. Ros said she snatched her keys from Vickie's hand and left, slamming the door behind her.

"Thank goodness I didn't have a spare set made from the dealership," Ros said. "It would have cost me $65 and I would have taken every cent out of Vickie's ass."

We discussed many things other than the Dunnam house during dinner: George's daughters, his new job, his old relationship and the new house he just purchased. Ros filled us in on her job and family and an upcoming trip she planned to England with her uncle. It was a welcomed and much-needed change. There was always so much going on with Edd, Beth and the activity in the home I was becoming consumed with the case. Not only was I loosing sleep over the events, but my every waking moment was focused on the activity: how to deal with it, how to keep the Dunnam's safe and sane, and how I could do more to help.

After dinner Ros and I cleared the table while George did dishes. I set out in search of a movie we hadn't seen or at least hadn't seen in a while. As I was looking through my several hundred movies, one jumped out at me, *The St. Francisville Experiment*. And I literally mean it jumped out at me. The video case fell off the shelf onto the floor at my feet. This must be the one, I decided. I know I wanted my mind off the Dunnam house, but this would be perfect. Not only would I show Ros and George how badly this film was done, but also, we could nit-pick at the researchers, who had only very brief training on equipment for the filming. This would be fun I thought. Ros and George agreed and we sat down to have a good laugh.

We first noticed the researchers were given a box of supplies for the night ahead of them. The box contained food, drinks, candles, flashlights, electronic equipment and an Ouija board! That should have been my first clue the producers hadn't told Troy Taylor the whole truth about the filming. I remembered something Edd and Beth had told me during my initial interview questions with them. They had used an Ouija board when they first moved into the house. I've known for a long time that using an Ouija board can open doorways to all kinds of nasty entities that generally don't like to leave. Because I was so distracted by the knocking sounds and all the other distracting activities, I completely forgot that they had told me this. Could this have started the activity at the Dunnam home? Did Edd and Beth open a doorway and allow something through that decided to stick around?

I grabbed the case file and began flipping through the papers until I found the initial interview question sheet. Sure enough, they had reported they had used an Ouija board when they first moved in. Beth wrote, "Edd finally asked it, 'If there are any ghosties that came through tonight that want to hang out with us, feel free.' Then we heard the knocking start on the living room wall for the first time. I got totally freaked out by it and made Edd get rid of the board the very next morning." Finally, something was beginning to make sense about the Dunnam house activities, I thought.

That night around midnight I heard an odd sound at my front door. Just once, not very loud, and it wasn't a knock or bang. To be quite honest it sounded like someone threw something small and hard at the center of the door. I saw no one on the porch through the peep-hole. I thought a bird had flown into the door or maybe the neighborhood rouges had thrown something at the door. When I finally opened the door, I saw a piece of decorative white marble resting on the doormat. My sidewalk had been lined with these stones years ago but most were buried under 18 inches of topsoil and grass, so I wasn't sure how this piece came to rest on the doormat. I didn't want to read too much into it, so I wrote it off as just a coincidence. I decided one of us entering the house had kicked it onto the porch and some noise only made it sound like someone had thrown it at my front door. I headed in to make fast friends with my pillow once again. This stone hitting the front door would become a nightly occurrence for the next several months.

Chapter Eight:
What New Things Would the New Year Bring?

New Year's Eve was uneventful. I've never been real big on celebrating a holiday were everyone sees how drunk they can get before proclaiming they will never do so again. Or they will eat so much they can barely walk before swearing they will loose those extra pounds in the upcoming year. People promise to give up or change many things about themselves at this time of year that are usually superficial. Being a person of strong moral convictions, I never make a promise I can't keep. Just ask my son. It just seems silly to me that I would make a promise to the most important person in my life, me, and then break it in just a few short days, weeks or months. For me, that begins a vicious cycle of self-loathing, self-esteem lowering or just plain guilt. I do stay up for a minute or so to watch the Times Square ball drop being from New York, but that's about all the effort I put into this holiday.

As the crowds on TV shouted "One," I heard the sound on my

front door again. Peering out the peep-hole, I saw no one. I slowly opened the door to discover another decorative white marble stone on the doormat. I placed a small jar on the porch to begin saving the stones. It now contained only two, but I suspected the number would grow. I jokingly thanked the gift giver and headed back for the comfort of my room.

I spent most of my night reviewing video and audio tapes recorded at the Dunnam house. I wondered how Edd and Beth were fairing on this night, usually festive for most. I hadn't heard from them and I took this as a good sign everything was quiet or at least fit into Edd's definition of "the usual." After midnight, I focused my attention on my upcoming inaugural ghost tour. I finished printing and filling out the invitations I would send out to my carefully chosen guinea pigs, I mean friends. These were people I knew I could trust to be truthful about the stories, the route lay-out, the length of the tour, and my delivery.

By 2:00 a.m., I still hadn't heard from Edd or Beth, so I assumed they had a quiet night and I decided to email them in the morning to see how their night went. I finished up my work, checked my emails and shut everything down for the night. I grabbed my dog and a sweet snack before curling up in bed, flipping through TV channels to see if there might be something interesting on. The guide rolled by with nothing on 279 of 280 channels. But a program about photography on The Learning Channel caught my eye. I knew chances were slim I would see anything about paranormal anomalies on program, but I might pick up some pointers on using film and camera equipment.

Just after 2:30 a.m. I heard Ros enter the front door. I heard her go into her bedroom and rustle around. She came into the kitchen and grabbed her bottle of spring water from the refrigerator before poking her head into my doorway.

"Hey dude, Happy New Year," she said.

"Happy New Year to you too, girl. How was work?" I asked.

"It was busy, full of belligerent customers all night, none of whom know the word 'tip' means 'leave cash for the woman behind the bar serving your ass,'" she answered.

"So busy, but not a money maker huh?" I commented.

Ros worked part-time as a local bartender and hated every minute of it. Although some nights an intelligent customer would begin an interesting conversation or the ghosts that resided in the bar would act up. Unfortunately these nights were few and far between.

"Nope," she answered. "Oh, before I forget," she paused, reaching into her pocket to pull out a piece of white marble, "this was on the porch step when I came in." She handed me the stone; another to add to the jar of mystery stones.

"It seems my new friend likes to play with rocks," I said. "I just hope who ever keeps tossing them at the door doesn't decide to start throwing them at the windows."

"Or passing cars," Ros added.

Ros sat down in the chair at my computer desk, lit a cigarette and leaned back to relax. As she looked at my TV, she quickly leaned the chair all the way forward.

"Oh my god dude," she said excitedly. "I was going to call you earlier and tell you to put this show on. But I was so busy, by the time I got a chance to call you; it was two hours after the show had ended."

"Oh, something interesting about this particular show Ros?" I asked.

"Yeah, actually the part coming up here in about two minutes," she replied. "This couple they are talking with," she said, pointing to the TV screen. "They have been going to this park in some part of this national forest for like 12 years or some such thing. Anyhow, every year that they visit, they take a photo in the same location on the side of this mountain thing near a waterfall and they always get this same weird thing that shows up in their picture of that spot; an upside-down rainbow"

I sat bolt upright in my bed, turned the TV volume up and leaned forward to focus my attention on the show. They interviewed a Native American shaman who said, "This phenomenon is rare, but does occur in certain locations where a doorway or portal to the spirit world exists. Science can't explain why this phenomenon shows up on film as the mysterious upside-down rainbow, but most shamans know the story from their ancestors. They tell of a warrior who remained to protect this world from spirits coming back through the doorway into this world. More than likely, the warrior has moved onto another plane of existence and left the doorway wide open for any spirit to come through to this side."

I sat there with my mouth hanging open. "Did I just hear that right?" I asked. "Did this guy just explain our upside-down rainbow as a real paranormal event?"

"Yep! That's exactly what you heard. I thought you'd love that," she replied excited.

"You can't even imagine how relieved I am to hear this" I said. "I'll make some phone calls tomorrow and see if anyone down here has ever heard of this anomaly occurring."

"Yeah, call your bud, you know, the Traditional Seminole guy you know," she answered.

"Hell yeah," I exclaimed. "He's my first phone call. I'm relieved, but still need some sort of documentation that this is what the Native Americans believe."

After Ros and I finished watching the show, she left for her bedroom after saying our good-nights. There was no way I was going to fall asleep. I went to the computer and started looking through the photos showing the upside-down rainbow. Every time we had been to the Dunnam home, we would get this same anomaly at the same location over the roof of the house, with the exception of one time. It didn't matter what direction the photo was taken from, the angle it was taken at, or even who took the photo, the rainbow was there at least once on every visit but once. The only time it wasn't present was on the day Vickie and the film crew were there. If I were to pick the best photo out of all of them, I would have to say the one showing Edd looking at the upside-down rainbow would have to be it!

I finally managed to get some sleep after tossing and turning for several hours. I was awakened in the morning early by the ringing phone. It was Beth.

"Dusty?" she asked.

"Morning Beth. How are things going?" I asked.

"All right I suppose, but I thought I should give you a call and update you on a few things," she said.

"By all means Beth, that's what I'm here for and what I need from you and Edd."

"Okay, thanks," she said. "I appreciate being able to tell someone about this stuff. It's really getting to me now. And just to let you know, it took me two tries to get through to you. The first try was static and then nothing. The second try, I got through."

"It seems you have better luck with getting me on the phone than Edd does," I said with a chuckle.

"It would seem that way, although after I didn't get through on the first try, I asked the spirits to let me call you and the call went right through."

"Maybe you should mention your method to Edd?" I replied. "See if it will work for him next time he tries to call me. So what's up Beth?"

"Do you remember me telling you about the child's voice singing over the baby monitor in the mornings?"

"Yes, I sure do."

"Well, it has gotten more frequent, every morning to be truthful," she continued. "And I think I finally figured out the song, although I don't know the name of it or the words to it."

"Oh? Can you explain that statement a little better Beth? You kind of lost me there."

"Sure Dusty," Beth said, laughing. "Have you ever seen the movie, *The Birds?*"

"Of course, a Hitchcock classic," I replied.

"When the kids are in the schoolhouse singing that song, blah, blah, blah, blah, blah, blah, round, round, round?" she continued. "Well, that's it. That's the song the little child's voice is singing over the baby monitor. I knew I had heard it before, but I couldn't put my finger on where or when. Then, last night, when I couldn't sleep with all the knocking and banging going on, I turned on the TV and there was *The Birds*. I had turned it on just as the children in the school were singing that song. I must have fallen asleep sometime during the movie because when I woke up still hearing the song, I rolled over and grabbed the remote to turn the TV off and discovered that it was all ready off and the same song was coming over the baby monitor."

"Damn Beth, that's an interesting way to figure out what you've been hearing for the past few months," I said. "Thanks for letting me know all of this."

"Sure thing Dusty, but that's not all," she continued. "Emily is talking to someone in her room all the time now. Edd and I can hear the voice, but when we open the door or get close to the door when it's open, the voice suddenly stops. It's really scary, gives me goosebumps just talking about it. Sometimes it's a woman's voice, but most of the time it's an indescribable voice, not really a man or a woman. And it's always so cold in there, especially in front of the closet door. Little Eddy is playing with something we can't see and we've seen the finger imprints rubbing his belly several more times in the past few days. That is so creepy!" She paused for a moment and then continued. "Oh, and before I forget, Edd has been seeing people walking through the house. He sits up all night in his chair in the living room watching them now. I sat up with him for a little while the other night and he was describing them to me as he saw them. It was too freaky for me! Dusty, I'm so scared about all this now. I never was before; maybe it's just the pregnancy. I don't know, but I am really scared."

"Okay Beth," I replied. "Take a deep breath. I know it's hard to deal with all this, even if you weren't pregnant. First thing is to tell Edd to call me and describe the people he's seeing; you don't need to be hearing about all that. Second thing, have you been lighting the candles and incense?"

"Yes, every night" she said. "It helps a lot for the first few hours, but then it seems to get worse after we go to bed. I don't want to leave anything burning when I'm in bed; you never know what might happen, especially with all that's all ready going on in this house."

"I can understand that Beth, probably a smart move," I replied. "Since Edd's already staying up, can't you have him keep an eye on the candles and incense?"

"I guess I could," she answered. "I'll ask him to do it tonight."

"Have you discussed what you want to do about the house and activity?" I continued.

"Well, I want to move, but Edd says we can't afford it right now. So I guess having you guys come over to cleanse the place would be a good start for now. We just need to wait on a move until after the baby arrives and we get a bit ahead from those bills."

"So you want us to come and do a cleansing?" I asked.

"Well, it's not definite yet, I'll have Edd call you in a day or so to let you know for sure," she answered.

"Okay Beth, just let me know," I said. "And you do know that you and Edd are invited for my first ghost tour right? Not to change the subject or anything."

"Oh, yes. I am looking forward to it. A whole evening out of the house with no kids and no ghosts, well, not these ghosts," she said, laughing.

"It's good to hear you laugh Beth," I commented.

"It feels good to laugh Dusty," she replied. "It's been a long time since I have. And Edd has changed so much, it's like he's obsessed with the ghosts. I feel like I can't talk to him anymore unless I talk to him about the ghosts."

"I know Beth. I've seen the changes in both of you. It's not your fault or Edd's; it's the activity in the house that is the cause of it all. You need to remember that. Just try to stay strong a little while longer and have Edd call me as soon as you decided what you both want to do. I really think since you can't afford to move right now that the sooner we start cleansing the house, the better it will be all around."

"I think so too," she agreed, "but getting Edd to commit to anything right now is like pulling teeth."

"Mention it to him when he gets home, Beth," I said. "Blame it on me bugging you if you want."

"Okay, thanks Dusty," she replied. "The last thing I need is to give him ammunition to start another silly argument over nothing."

"Exactly," I agreed. "Okay Beth. You take care and call me day or night, if you need anything."

"I will Dusty. Like I said, I'm really scared now. So you will be hearing from me more often, I promise." Beth hung up.

I started my day with coffee and phone calls. My first call was to the Traditional Seminole Nation to see if anyone might have heard of the upside-down rainbow anomaly. My hopes were not high after I began making my calls. My friend in the Nation was away for several weeks and no one was quite sure how to get in touch with him. I finally spoke with a young woman whose father was a shaman. She agreed the upside-down rainbow was a portal for spirits to pass through. She told me there should be a warrior guarding the portal so nothing negative could come from the other side to this side. The woman said many Native Americans had similar beliefs in their traditions. I asked her if this belief was written down, like the similarities between the Native American tale of Hiawatha and the Bible story of Jonah and the whale. She replied it had been told to her by her father, and it had been narrated to him by his father. She did recall something written from the Hope Tribe, but she couldn't be more specific. Many Native Americans have oral traditions so many of their tales and histories were never transcribed.

My next call was to my ex-husband's Cherokee Nation family. I was told the same thing about the upside-down rainbow. I managed to find an obscure reference to the anomaly on a website for the Hope Tribe and emailed the site's webmaster to try to find the story in written form, but never received a response.

This was too much. How lucky we were to have stumbled onto this information, I thought. Since I already knew there had been several tribes in the vicinity of were the Dunnam house now stood, this made complete sense to me; well, as much sense as an anomaly like this could make. If nothing else, it might help explain the amount of activity going on in their home. If the portal was wide open, why wouldn't every entity want to return to this side for another look-around? I felt like I was reaching a bit, but it was the first corroborated piece of evidence we had, no matter how bizarre it sounded.

The next few days saw no contact from the Dunnams. I decided if I hadn't heard from them by the end of the week I would call to see how things were going. I knew they were probably busy with after-holiday chores and preparing for the arrival of the newest member of the family. I busied myself with preparations for the upcoming tour and reviewing video and audio tapes from their house. There were some interesting anomalies on the video tapes, but nothing that really impressed me. An orb here and there, a flash of light, the cat watching something I couldn't see and some bizarre interference that looked like a rainbow was all I saw.

The audio tapes however, were awesome. The number of voices speaking at the same time was so great I couldn't make out individuals. They overlapped in so many spots it was like listening to a cocktail party from just outside the room. The tapes captured the banging sounds, the knocking sounds, a few high-pitched screams and moans, the heavy dragging sound, the galloping horse sound and even the child singing. It took several days of repeated listening to note everything on them. The final list of sound anomalies from the two 90-minute tapes came to nearly 17 pages so I didn't include it in this book.

My midnight visitor continued to leave a rock on my front doorstep every night. I had by now collected over a dozen stones in the jar and expected more. Most nights, just one stone was left but other nights, as many as three stones would be sitting on my doormat when I opened the door. I still wasn't sure if this event was somehow linked to the activity at the Dunnam house, but I had a strong feeling it was. I never mentioned this activity to Edd or Beth. I didn't want them to feel guilt or have any other bad feelings for me being stupid or forgetful enough to drag one of their "ghosties" home with me, if it was truly related to the activities at their home. Some professional I turned out to be, I thought. This was my fault, not theirs. I took full responsibility for not cleansing myself and car before I left their home, no matter how upset I was. Their plates were full enough without me burdening them with this little problem of mine.

During this quiet time I received an email from a woman named Janet who professed to be a "gifted sensitive." We chatted back and forth via email several times, and I finally spoke with her on the 'phone. I was careful to not discuss the Dunnam case and our theories of what may be intruding into this world. She seemed to be knowledgeable in demonology and said she had been doing work as a sensitive for many years. She told me she would like to visit the Dunnam household so she could show me just how gifted she was. We shall see, I thought as I invited her along to our next visit.

I received an email from Edd on Jan. 4 relaying the same activities

Beth had shared with me three days earlier. He went into greater detail about the apparitions he had seen. There were five men, four women, two children and one thing he described as a "big blob of brownish mud." I assumed he was speaking of the "Mud Man" he had briefly mentioned about three months into our investigation. We had yet to see or photograph any of these apparitions; we were only going on what Edd told us.

Edd described Mud Man as being a big blob of mud shaped like a man but hunched over; very primal in nature. Mud Man was heavy and dark and was, by Edd's account, the cause of the heavy galloping sounds across the roof of their home. Edd felt he and Mud Man had a special understanding: Edd would see Mud Man, Mud Man would taunt Edd, Edd would yell at Mud Man, Mud Man would make loud noises and move heavy objects to be mischievous, Edd would shout obscenities at Mud Man, and Mud Man would apparently tire of the game and stomp away loudly towards one side of the roof. Edd would be left frustrated and angry and Mud Man would not return for the remainder of the night. This same scenario would repeat several times and was relayed by Edd, Beth, two different neighbors, and two of my researchers. This was one Dunnam home entity I didn't want to experience first-hand. I printed Edd's email and placed it in the Dunnam case file.

It was Jan. 7 before Edd called. "Hey kiddo! How's the New Year treating you," he said.

"So far, so good Edd," I answered, "how about you?"

"Pretty good," he said, "still kind of freaky around here. Things seem to be getting worse and worse, so Beth and I wanted to know when you guys could come out and do this cleansing thing?"

"Let me see, how is the ninth for you?" I asked.

"Perfect! What time?"

"How's five o'clock?"

"Sounds good kiddo! You guys gonna stay all night?" Edd asked.

"We can Edd," I replied. "Would you like us to?"

"Sure, that would be great."

"Everything else all right Edd?"

"Yep, as good as can be. So, we'll see you day after tomorrow kiddo."

"Okay Edd, see you then."

That was the shortest phone call I ever had with Edd. Something wasn't right, I wasn't sure what, but I just knew something wasn't right. Edd's phone call ate at me for about an hour and I finally called back to make sure everyone was all right. It took me several tries to get through before I finally got Beth on Edd's cell phone. They were visiting neighbors for dinner and a card game. I felt really stupid calling thinking something was wrong, when they were trying to have a bit of normalcy in their lives. I apologized to Beth for the intrusion. She thanked me for my concern. She said she was actually glad I called because they were having a lousy time and my call gave them an excuse to leave. They already had a baby sitter, so she and Edd would go out and try to forget about the house for a few hours. It sounded like an awesome plan to me, I told her.

I emailed the group to see who would be available to assist with the cleansing on Jan. 9. I then gathered up the items I knew we'd need to perform the cleansing process at the Dunnam home. I packed lots of white candles, both votive and seven-day, plenty of frankincense and myrrh incense cones, a bag of White Sage, sea salt, spring water and even Holy Water, just in case.

My personal spiritual beliefs have no bearing on our efforts to remove spirits from a client's home. However, the clients' spiritual beliefs can influence our methods. I urge clients to allow us to use the basics, things we know work well with any given situation. Say we're dealing with a human spirit whose spiritual beliefs were Buddhist. It is doubtful Holy Water would work. But sometimes the clients' personal beliefs play into the way they want the job done. We try to comply with the clients wishes while doing what we know is effective. We do not normally promote this service. Instead, we reserve this service for only extreme situations because the physical, psychological and emotional drain can be intense on each of us participating in the cleansing. In the case of Edd and Beth who had become like family to us, we knew they would be open to whatever could be done. After all, their case did fit into the extreme category.

Chapter Nine:
Bring on the Tylenol!
The Cleansing is About to Begin!

Before I begin to write about the happenings during the first cleansing of the Dunnam home, I would like to say this is not a process that should be done by anyone without adequate knowledge to perform a spiritual cleansing. If such a cleansing is attempted without knowing how to respond to anything that may arise, dangerous results may occur. By dangerous, I mean the possibility of attracting more unwanted spiritual guests or creating spontaneous fires, power outages, phone or Internet problems or even physical harm to the clients and the people doing the cleansings. Put simply: Do not attempt this at home. While our cleansing seemed to go well, we'd have to wait to see what would happen over the next few days. The spirits did seem to want the living gone from their space. Remember, there are no experts. No one can ever be sure of exactly what will happen when dealing with the paranormal.

I started to mentally and physically prepare myself for what I knew was to come. The stress and utter exhaustion a body experiences after doing a full cleansing of a paranormally active home can take days to recover physically and longer mentally if you are not properly prepared.

I called my friend and spiritual mentor, Deborah to seek her advice on the current situation at the Dunnam home. I went over my plans with her, and she agreed with the methods I had chosen to use. She asked several questions to assure we would be prepared and safe throughout the cleansing. I've known Deborah and her husband Gene for several years and they have taught me a great deal about myself and my spirituality. I have come to think of them as family and Deborah has always been there for me when I needed help with any situation I had gotten into. She also recommended I call a mutual friend of ours, Hazel, who was the head Reverend at the Cassadaga Spiritualist Camp.

It took several tries for me to finally reach the busy Hazel by phone. Since assuming her role as spiritual leader of the camp, she was an in demand woman, with good reason. Hazel knows her metaphysical and spiritual stuff and has always been great to talk to when you need a friendly ear. We discussed other ways of dealing with the activities. Hazel recommended bringing drums or bells to make a lot of noise to "shake them loose from the area." She also mentioned a way to remove negative energy with an egg, adding it was generally done in an only unoccupied location. I thanked her for the advice and told her I'd keep her posted. She also reminded me of the problems we could all face if we weren't prepared for the cleansing. I told her I knew of the dangers, that we would all take every step we could to be safe both mentally and physically.

I knew I could not bring the entire research group to help with the cleansing. I also knew I would need healthy and emotionally stable people along; no one with a cold or other significant issues. They might be distracted from the cleansing and we could all suffer because of it. I chose Kristi, Suzi and Ros. I knew with Kristi's Christian background, Suzi's Native American background and the knowledge Ros and I had of New Age cleansing we would be just fine. My main hope was to rid the home of the unwanted and increasingly unruly guests. Even if we could calm the activities down enough so the family wasn't frightened and could get some decent sleep, I would have been content.

We arrived at the Dunnam home just after 5:00 p.m. We didn't bring the usual cases of equipment, just a couple of grocery bags containing the items we would need for the cleansing. We greeted Edd and Beth. They returned the greetings and began to recount their recent occurrences. It had actually been quieter than before and I began to wonder if we even needed to do a cleansing. I told Beth that she would need to accompany us because there were things she would need to do each day after we left.

Ros began to light the White Sage. She first placed a handful of the dried leaves into a fireproof container and set them ablaze. The smoke billowed around her as she blew onto the smoldering leaves gently. She cleansed each of us in turn before we turned our attention to the house itself. I mixed together spring water and sea salt as Suzi rang bells and beat on the walls to "shake them loose" as Hazel had suggested. Kristi sprinkled us with Holy water and began to light white candles throughout the house.

Beth followed Ros and I around, asking questions. It amazed me how open minded she was being about having these lunatics in her home doing things most people would never permit. Ros lead, using the wafting White Sage smoke to permeate every corner of the house. I followed, sprinkling the sea salt and spring water mixture in every corner. Kristi lit tons of white candles while reciting St. Michael's Prayer and sprinkling Holy water all around.

Things were quiet at first; too quiet, I thought to myself. With all the activity that had been going on in this house, why had they now chosen to be quiet? Was the cleansing working? Were they hiding in wait? Were they leaving without putting up a fight? Since no two cases are ever the same, it is hard to know what to expect, especially when cleansing. I decided to just keep a positive outlook as I continued the work, repeatedly telling myself the spirits were leaving and the family would get back to a more normal existence.

It took us about three hours to finish walking through the house. When we finished, we cleansed ourselves and Edd and Beth again before sitting down in the living room for a deserved break before the next round of cleansing. I lit a cigarette and guzzled an ice-cold Mt. Dew. Everyone else began to relax and catch their breath. Edd and Beth sat quietly while Suzi opened a Pepsi and munched on Doritos, Kristi sipped on water, and Ros made her way to the rest room.

I invited Janet, the supposed gifted psychic, to join us on this night and asked her to arrive at eight o'clock. She quietly knocked on the door, made her introduction, and began to tell us her impressions of the home. I was not impressed with her impressions. She misread every aspect of the activity we had documented to date. I thanked her for her time and showed her to the door post-haste before we all focused on her impressions more so than the job at hand.

As we sat quietly trying to focus positive thoughts on the activity being gone from the home, the living room suddenly got very cold. I looked at Suzi and Kristi and I saw they had noticed the temperature drop as well. Two of the white candles Kristi had lit earlier extinguished simultaneously when Ros bolted out of the bathroom.

"Dude," she said. "You're not going to believe this, but I was sitting in the bathroom tending to business, and I felt like someone was watching me. All of a sudden the shower curtain blew open, like someone was in there with me."

"Are you all right?" Kristi asked.

"Yeah, just a bit shaken," Ros replied.

"Guess they aren't gone," I said. "We should start again"

Everyone agreed and Kristi and Suzi headed for the hallway bathroom. Kristi sprinkled Holy water as she made her way through the doorway, then yelled back to Ros. "Did you move this candle while you were in here Ros?"

"No, why," Ros replied.

"It's sitting in the sink," she said.

"What?" Ros exclaimed. "No, I didn't touch it. It was on the counter top when I was so rudely interrupted."

We slowly worked our way through the house again, repeating

the same steps we had taken just a few hours earlier. While I was in Edd and Beth's bedroom, Little Eddy ran down the hall into the bedroom before doing a one-eighty and barking at the hallway. I poked my head out but didn't see anything. I also didn't notice any temperature changes or anything else out of the ordinary. But Little Eddy continued barking for about 20 minutes. No matter what we did to try to quiet him, he kept looking at the hallway and barking. Other than that incident, the second attempt at cleansing the home was uneventful. We all hoped this was a good sign.

We took another short break without interruption from the "ghosties" this time, and everyone noticed the whole house seemed to actually *feel* better. By "feeling" I mean in a sixth-sense sort of way. It isn't something you can see or touch, but something you feel in you psyche, in your guts, down deep in your soul. The sense of dread and heavy feeling in the house had lessened greatly. It wasn't completely gone, but there was a noticeable improvement.

After about 20 minutes, we decided it was time to make our third and final cleansing pass of the night. I made sure Beth was with me as this was her last opportunity to watch the cleansing process. As she would need to keep this up on her own, I wanted to be sure she had the routine and order down pat. She never uttered a word as we walked through her home. Instead, she had a look both of fascination and fear the whole time. It was an odd look, but one I would come to know well over the years as we dealt with frightened homeowners as we performed the cleansing process. Most afflicted homeowners want to be rid of paranormal activities, but without doing any of the work. I try to explain to them I cannot be with them on a 24/7 basis, they need to do this themselves. Most times they halfheartedly do the cleansing work for a week or so and then stop it altogether. That's when I get another call that the activity increased again. Fortunately Beth was not like this. She had a genuine interest in protecting her home and family, and I knew she would not be a slacker when it came to cleansing her home. She had all ready purchased the necessary supplies and was asking all the right questions as she walked beside me. She had all ready begun the process by lighting the candles and incense every night. These were all good signs this would work out for the best. That was my hope.

When we had finished the third part of the cleansing I sat with Edd and Beth as the others packed up and went outside to cleanse themselves before we left. I explained to Beth how important it was to keep up with this same routine every night. I left them the supplies leftover from the night and began to cleanse them and myself before saying goodnight.

"Do either of you notice a change?" I asked.

"I do Dusty. It feels lighter in here, if that makes sense," Beth replied.

"That makes perfect sense to me Beth and it's a good thing," I said, smiling.

"I can't feel or see any of them in here anymore" Edd added. "It feels like they have all moved outside somewhere and are waiting. Am I crazy?"

"No Edd," I said. "You're not crazy. That is what you should feel. They are waiting, waiting to come back inside once your defenses are down. This is why it is so important to keep up with this every night. The longer you keep the defenses up, the quicker they will realize they are not wanted here and they will move on, either to their rest or onto another location, hopefully the former."

"I finally feel like I can get a good night's sleep," Beth said.

"I hope you can Beth," I said. "I'm sure you need it. Could you hit the record button on the VCR in Emily's room tonight before you go to bed?"

"Sure thing," she replied. "We will see you tomorrow night for your inaugural tour and I'll bring it with me, if that's alright?"

"Great! I do appreciate it," I said. "And I'm glad that you'll both be getting a night out of the house, not that ghosts are what you'd like to be dealing with on your night out," I added with a laugh.

"That's what we understand now Dusty," Edd said. "We're glad you invited us. We're actually looking forward to it."

"Okay then," I said, "I'll see you both tomorrow night at 7:30. Please have a good night and let me know how things go. Don't forget the routine tonight Beth and if you need me for anything, just call."

"I will Dusty," Beth replied. "Thanks again."

As I headed out the front door I felt a sense of calm for the first time in the Dunnam house. Just two feet away from the porch however didn't feel calm. I could feel the heaviness in the air surrounding the house. I could feel "them" watching me. I could almost see Mud Man sitting on the peak of the roof staring down at me. I felt unnerved as I got into my car. I spoke aloud my protection, "No spirits may follow me home!" as I closed the car door and turned the ignition key.

The drive home was long and quiet. Everyone was exhausted. A couple of them dozed off while the others stared quietly into the darkness outside the car windows. I was so tired I couldn't even form a thought about anything that had happened that evening. I turned the radio up loud, set the AC on "ice" and hoped I could stay awake long enough to get us back to Daytona safely.

When I arrived home I checked the answering machine and emails for messages from Edd or Beth. There were none. Which I took as being a very good sign, things were quiet at the Dunnam home.

I went to bed trying to think of all the stories I would be telling the next night on the first official ghost tour and I kept thinking how ironic it was to be telling stories about true hauntings to people who were having their own experiences. I was sad as I lay there trying to fall asleep. I wondered how many people lived in these situations everyday and just wrote them off as imagination or as themselves being crazy. I know not everyone is a believer, but to live with fear on a daily or nightly basis would drive anyone insane!

Chapter Ten:
The First Tour and more,
MUCH MORE!

The morning of Jan. 10 was as hectic as any other morning: answering phone calls, responding to emails, feeding the dogs, getting Kyle off to school and the usual four zillion other things I do every morning. Edd or Beth still had contacted me, which I continued to take as a good sign. I hoped they both finally got a good night's sleep and they would tell me as much when I saw them that evening.

I was pretty nervous all day. Even though this was a test tour with my closest friends, I wanted them to enjoy it. The thought that it might be horrible kept eating away at me. I tried to convince myself that it was going to be a great tour. I had all the scripts down pat, the documentation had been done properly, the history had been researched in great detail, and I knew I could tell the stories in a fun, interesting and informative way. None of that mattered though, I was still nervous as hell.

I ate a little around 4:00 p.m. and lay down for a quick pre-tour nap. When I got up I showered and dressed. I wore my favorite black velvet gothic outfit with an accompanying red cloak, comfy shoes and slung a small handbag over my shoulder to carry my cheat sheets in case I needed them. I packed the sale items, T-shirts, booklets and refrigerator magnets into a box, grabbed my lantern and nervously waited for seven o'clock to arrive.

Suzi arrived just before 7:00 and made me change my socks. I was wearing thick comfy brown socks and she told me they would look silly; I should but on a black pair. I changed my socks and smoked another cigarette before Suzi, Ros and I loaded into the car for the 10-minute drive to the tour departure location. I was so nervous I could barely speak. Suzi and Ros tried to calm me by making jokes and talking about subjects to take my mind off my haywire nerves. It wasn't until Suzi talked to me about the Dunnam house that I finally began to settle down.

I know it was an odd way to settle down, talking about a haunted house that was the most frightening experience I had to date in my life. Being in that house and hearing the noises, sounds and voices, watching things move or pets being petted may not sound like a lot to an outsider, but I got to the point I needed to be convinced to go back to that house. I don't mind dealing with things I can see, but when something throws a set of golf clubs at you and injures your body, that's when fear takes over. Since that event, I waited for another injury either to myself or another member of the group every time I walked into that house. I readily admit that I had become afraid to be in that house.

My nervousness about the tour turned to the fear I felt at the Dunnam home: great distraction technique Suzi! It worked like a charm and as I waited for tour guests to arrive, I was no longer nervous.

I remembered I had not heard from Edd and Beth since the previous night when Edd and Beth finally pulled up. Edd jumped out in his usual extraverted way. "Dusty! How ya doin' kiddo? Great night for hunting some ghosties." He laughed.

"Edd, you crazy son of a bitch. How are you?" I responded,

laughing.

"I feel great," he said enthusiastically. "Had the best nights sleep in nearly eight months last night, with no interruptions from our spirited friends." He laughed again.

"Really? That's wonderful," I said, relieved. "I am so glad the cleansing helped. How is Beth?"

Just then Beth stepped out of the passenger side of the minivan. "I'm fine Dusty," she said. "I slept great too! What a difference. I feel almost reborn."

"Awesome! I am so happy for you," I replied.

Beth handed me two video tapes with dates, times and locations hand-written on the boxes and labels. She explained the one was recorded a few days ago and she had misplaced it somehow, but the other was from last night. I took both tapes and placed them into my car. Edd fiddled around in the back of the van before he suddenly emerged with a horse skull. "Here kiddo, this is for you," he announced.

"Gee Edd, thanks. This is for me?" I asked.

"Yep, been sitting in our backyard since we moved in," he answered. "I know you like this kind of stuff, so I figured you would give it a good home."

"Wow! Thanks Edd," I said as I put the skull in the trunk of the car and told everyone to follow as the tour began. Eleven out of 15 people were able to attend. When I realized the amount of people attending, my nerves went coo-coo again.

I walked them all to the northwest corner of the Main Street and Peninsula Drive intersection and began the tour.

"Greetings and Welcome to Haunts of the World's Most Famous Beach ghost tours," I spoke loudly. "My name is Dusty and I'll be your tour guide tonight. This is the first and only ghost tour on the east coast of the United States to be owned and operated by a certified ghost hunter and active certified paranormal researcher."

It was then I noticed they were all mesmerized. I had a willing yet captive audience and they were all enjoying themselves only four sentences into the tour. This was great! And now I could finally calm down and focus on the telling of the haunting tales that had taken three years to research and document.

The first three stories went very well. Everyone was taking photos and getting some good paranormal results. They were getting orbs and energy ribbons, vortexes and the EMFs were going off with frequent high readings. I was ecstatic.

When I finished telling the eighth story, I introduced Edd and Beth as my honored guests. Edd began to recount a few of the other-worldly experiences they had at their home. The focus was on him for nearly 15 minutes and everyone stared at him like they were deer in headlights. Edd, of course, was eating up the attention and playing off his fears in a jovial way. It was so "Edd" of him to do it that way.

When he finished, the group began to move to the spot for the next story. As I walked in the lead I could hear the others behind asking Edd and Beth about the experiences they were having in their home. Beth seemed to shy away from the questions. After all, this was her first night away from it all in months and I was sure she didn't want to be reminded of it. Edd however, was in his glory. Here were several people that had never been to his home he could talk to without concern. It was very therapeutic for him.

During the second to last story about the World Famous Boot Hill Saloon, I mentioned the owners and management offered a drink special to our tour guests after the tour. Edd got very excited and asked others in the group to join him after the tour. He snagged only two takers, and feeling sorry for him, Ros and I joined Edd and Beth for a short while after the tour.

When the tour ended the entire group applauded me. I was embarrassed but proud. They purchased several T-shirts and books and took as many business and rack cards as they could to help promote Daytona Beach's newest attraction. I thanked them all for coming and for their honest critiques of the tour and said good-bye to each one of them.

Ros, Edd and Beth and I drove our vehicles the 50 yards to the Boot Hill Saloon's parking lot and went inside. Edd swaggered up to the main bar and came back with a pitcher of beer and iced teas for

Beth and I. The regular kind of iced tea, not the alcohol infused Long Island kind. He began getting loud, telling jokes and challenging us all to games of pool. At first we played partners but I then accepted his offer as a single challenge. During Edd's turn I spoke with Beth. She seemed unusually quiet. I wondered if she really had gotten a good night's sleep or if being around the ghost stories all evening was just keeping her mind on the events in her own home. She talked a bit about Emily and her anticipations of the new baby, but didn't speak of the activity at the home. I decided not to push the subject as this was her first night out in months and I really didn't want her to focus on the house while she was out.

After I had beaten Edd at the pool table several times, Ros and I made our exit. Edd wanted us to stay, but we could tell Beth was ready to head home. Being eight months pregnant tends to tire a person out quickly. As I got into my car I noticed Edd and Beth leaving as well. I guess she talked him into heading home before he got tipsy. The ride home for them was about a half an hour on the interstate and wasn't a good place to be sober, and definitely not drunk.

As soon as I got in the door of the house I peeled off my outfit and got into some very comfortable clothes. I grabbed a cold soda and headed off into my bedroom to watch the video filmed the night before Beth had given me. I then realized that Beth had given me two tapes and decided to watch the one that was recorded prior to January 9 last. I wanted to see if the cleansing had made a difference in the home. Ros stayed to watch it with me and sat next to me in front of the television.

As soon as the video tape started we saw Beth backing away from the VCR. She left the room for a moment and reentered with Emily on her hip. We watched her change Emily's diaper and play with her for a few minutes on the changing table. They were both in good spirits and Emily was cooing and giggling with her mother. It was a sweet thing to watch after all the bad things we had seen and experienced in that house. One would never know that there had been anything but happy memories being made in the home.

At 19 minutes and 28 seconds into the recording, we watched Beth lay Emily down in her crib and give her a nighttime bottle. Beth turned on a music box hanging on the side of the crib before leaning over to kiss her sleepy baby good night. The overhead light went off in the room and the camera night vision adjusted to the reduced light source. Once the camera focused in again, I turned the volume up full on the television set. If we were going to hear anything, this would be the time.

We could hear Emily sucking on her bottle, the music coming from the music box, and we heard Emily occasionally rolling over in her crib. The music box began to slow and the pace of Emily's bottle sucking slowed in pace with it. I could tell she was reaching the point of solid sleep when we heard the most unnerving thing I have ever and hope will ever hear.

A voice called out, "Oh Emme!" This was not a male or female, it was something in between. Ros and I both got goose bumps and cold chills as we watched in horror the following video footage. Emily sat up in her crib quickly and said, "Uh huh?" looking towards her closet door. She then stood up and held the side rail on the crib and watched something we couldn't see at first as it moved from the front of the closet door to the front of her changing table. That was when we saw the object. A large gray blob floated across the room and hovered directly in front of Emily in her crib.

"Uh huh…No…No…aww," Emily said to the object. Emily was responding to this blob. Ros and I sat there watching with our mouths hanging open. I couldn't believe what we were seeing. Emily could see and hear this gray blob and they were having a sort of other-worldly conversation. Normally I would have rewound the tape to have a second, third of even thirtieth look, but I couldn't push the rewind button. I had to keep watching to see what would come next.

Emily giggled a couple of times, pointed at her stuffed animals and then sat down in the crib. The crib began to violently slam up against the bedroom wall. The gray blob then moved down over the top of Emily and she began to scream, "No! No! No! NO!!!" She cried in terror, I mean real terror, as this thing seemed to sit on top of her. After several minutes it disappeared, but Emily kept on screaming. She screamed so loud the speakers on my television cut out. This was horrifying. I'm a mom and know the difference between the 'I have a wet diaper' cry, the 'I want to get back up' cry, the 'I want a bottle' cry, and this was none of those. This was terror, sheer terror. My heart sank as I listened to her screams.

Ros and I both began to cry. Here we were watching this helpless innocent baby being attacked by something and we couldn't do anything about it. The incident was now in the past. There was no going back. Why didn't I see this coming? How could I have left that baby in that house without any special protection? How many times had she been through this and no one noticed? How was I going to tell Edd and Beth their baby daughter had been terrified and attacked by an entity in her own crib? Why didn't they hear it? Why didn't they come to her aid? Was this entity able to manipulate the sound of Emily's screams so her own parents couldn't hear her? The guilt that ran through me was overwhelming. Any parent who saw that footage would feel the exact same way. I decided right then and there Edd and Beth, especially Beth, would never, and I do mean never see this footage. The psychological ramifications would be immeasurable.

After watching another 30 minutes and not seeing any other activity accept for Emily screaming in terror and occasionally calling out for her Mommy and Daddy, I called Edd and Beth, hoping they had made it home all ready. Ros stayed in the room and turned the volume down and continued to watch the tape as I made my phone call.

The phone rang several times and finally Edd answered. "Hello?"

"Edd? It's Dusty," I said. "I need to speak with you right away."

"Okay kiddo, what's up?" he replied.

"I just watched the video tape that Beth gave me tonight that was taped last night in Emily's room and I need for you to get Emily out of that room."

"What? Why? What happened? What did you see?"

"Are you sitting down Edd?" I asked.

"Yeah, why? Do I need to be?" he asked.

"Yes," I replied. "It's not good Edd. I don't know how to put this gently, so I'm just going to say it. Emily was attacked in her crib by an entity."

"What," Edd shouted into the phone. "Say that again! I know I didn't hear what you just said!"

"Yes you did Edd," I continued. "I said Emily was attacked in her crib. You need to get her out of that room and not let her sleep in there anymore. We need to come back down and cleanse the Hell out of that room."

"Which tape was it?" Edd asked.

"The one Beth taped last night. Did you hear Emily crying at all last night?" I asked.

"Yeah right after Beth put her down to sleep we heard her pouting for about 10 minutes, but we just thought she wanted to get back up since you guys had just left," he explained. "She quieted down and we didn't hear her again until this morning when she came over the baby monitor crying to get her diaper changed and get out of the crib."

"How was she today? Did you notice anything strange about her?" I asked.

"Beth noticed a couple of bruises on her back and legs, but she thought they were from Emily rolling around in the crib. We have heard her roll so hard that the crib hits the wall and makes a loud thumping sound."

"When have you heard this Edd?" I asked, concerned.

"A few times over the past couple of months," he answered. "Didn't really think anything of it 'cause she does it a lot."

"Jesus! Edd, it may not have been Emily trying to get your attention," I said. "It may have been this thing in her room attacking her. Get her out of there. I'm on my way over."

"Okay Dusty," he said. "We'll see you in a few. I'm gonna start breaking down the crib now."

I hung up the phone and grabbed my keys. I told Ros I was going to go over to Edd and Beth's and not to wait up for me. Ros told me she would watch the rest of the tape and if she saw anything else she felt I needed to know about right away, she would call my cell phone. I grabbed a couple of sodas and an extra pack of smokes and headed out the door.

I drove like a bat out of hell on Interstate 4 all the way to Deltona. Once, I looked down at the speedometer and saw I was doing 103 miles per hour. I backed it off to 80 and hit the cruise control. If a law enforcement officer had stopped me, I don't think they would have believed that I was on my way to a haunted house to help protect a baby. I wasn't even sure that was what I was doing. Why was I going over there? Edd could have moved Emily out of that room without any help from me. Maybe it was the guilt I was feeling? Maybe it was my nurturing, mothering nature coming out? Maybe I just needed to see with my own eyes that the crib had been moved? I really don't know what my true reason was, but I do know that I had to go to that house that night.

When I arrived at the Dunnam house on Hancock Road, I knocked on the door and I heard a voice from within calling me to come in. I entered the house and saw no one in the living room but could hear voices at the back of the house I assumed in Edd and Beth's bedroom. I made my way down the hall and made a quick stop by Emily's room. It was hot and there was still no echo in the room. The crib was gone and so were some of Emily's toys. The closet door was ajar and when I went to open it further and look inside I was overwhelmed with a feeling of dread. I removed my hand from the closet doorknob and left the room.

I made my way down the hall into Edd and Beth's bedroom to find Beth and her niece holding up two ends of the crib while Edd was tightening the bolts on one of the side rails. They had three sides nearly together and the forth side rail lay on the floor on the other side of Edd and Beth's queen size bed.

"Gimme a second kiddo," Edd said. "As soon as I tighten this last bolt I'll take a quick break and you can fill us in on what you saw on the tape."

"That's fine Edd," I replied. "Take your time. How you holding up Beth?"

"I was fine until your phone call Dusty," Beth replied. "I thought we had finally gotten a handle on this mess. Now I'm scared to death. All I want to do is leave this house and never come back."

"I can understand you feeling that way Beth," I said. "And that may wind up being your final option with all of this. If I would have known anything even remotely like this was going on, I would have gotten you all out of here long ago."

"It's that bad?" she asked.

"Yeah Beth, it's that bad," I replied.

Just then Little Eddy raced into the room closely followed by Emily who was giggling in delight. Little Eddy ran under the bed and Emily hung off the end of it with a look on her face like she had just won a magnificent prize. Little Eddy continued to bark while Emily giggled and laughed. Her jovial mood was a nice distraction from the horror I had witnessed on my VCR just minutes before.

We giggled along with her until we heard Little Eddy begin to growl. Emily stood at the end of the bed and lifted the bed skirt to look for the puppy. She tossed the bed skirt down quickly and stood upright with a look of fear on her face. As she began to walk slowly towards the hallway the fourth side of the crib lifted off the floor and flew over Edd and Beth's bed to come to rest on top of Emily, pinning her to the floor.

Edd dropped his tools and raced to help his child. Beth squeezed out from behind the nearly completed crib to follow. I crossed the room to help. Beth's niece stood up against the wall screaming. It took all three of us nearly a minute to finally pry the crib rail off the screaming Emily, although it seemed more like hours while we struggled and listened to her screaming in fear and pain. When we finally got the rail off of her, she had all ready begun to bruise. Long bluish-green lines had started to appear on her back, arms and legs in an odd diagonal pattern.

"Oh my God, Edd. We need to take her to the hospital," Beth screamed.

"Beth? I know this is going to sound cruel, but you can't do that," I said.

"Why not?" Beth exclaimed. "She is obviously hurt bad. I can't just leave her like this. What if something is broken?"

"I know I'm not a doctor, but I seriously doubt anything is broken," I answered. "If you take her to the emergency room, what are you going to tell the doctor's there, that a ghost attacked your baby? They will take her away from you for child abuse so fast you won't know what hit you. Think about it Beth. You know I'm right. We'll just get some ice to put on the bruises and you can give her some children's Tylenol for the pain. I know she's your daughter, but I wish you'd consider what I'm saying."

This may seem cruel of me, but I had experience with emergency room doctors in similar situations before. I knew what the outcome would be.

"I'll get the ice," Beth's niece cried out.

"Beth, listen to her," Edd said. "You know she's right. We've been through so much, Mama. If we take her to the emergency room and loose custody of her, even temporarily, it would kill us both. Let's do what Dusty said and see how she is in the morning. Please baby."

"Morning? Morning?" Beth shouted as she clung to her crying baby. "I am not staying in this house another minute. I'll agree to not taking her to the emergency room, but you find a way to get her and I out of this house tonight Edd. I mean now. Tonight."

"I'm going to call your parents and see if you and Emily can go stay there until I can find us a new house to live in," Edd said.

"Do you mean it Edd?" Beth said in obvious relief. "I really can't stay here any longer. I'll go crazy. And I can't bring another baby into this house, not with what's going on here."

"I'm making the phone call now Mama," Edd said. "You all come out into the living room and take care of Emily while I talk with your Mom and Dad."

Edd scooped Emily up as I helped Beth off the floor and we went into the living room. Beth sat on the couch and Edd handed his still crying daughter over to her who began to snuggle with her and hum into her ear. Beth's niece appeared with three small ice packs wrapped in dish towels and Beth gently applied them to her daughter's bruised body. Beth cried as she tried to soothe Emily's own cries.

"No, you don't understand," Edd shouted in the kitchen. "This is not a joke. I am beggin' you to get Beth and Emily a plane ticket and get them out of this house before one of them gets killed. This is serious. Dusty has it on video tape of this thing attacking Emily in her crib. I'm not kiddin'. I need you to help me keep my family safe until I can find another house for us to move into." There was a short pause in Edd's speaking, then he began again, "Okay, okay. Thank you. I owe you big time for this. I'll be waiting for your call. Thanks again. Bye."

"Edd, what happened?" Beth asked. "What did they say?"

"I can't believe it," Edd answered, annoyed. "They stayed here. They saw and heard things and they didn't believe me when I told them what had just happened."

"Do you want me to talk to my Mom Edd?" Beth asked.

"No Mama," he replied. "It's okay now. Your Mom is going to call and get you and Emily on the first available flight up there and you two will stay with them until I can get us moved to a safe house."

"That's good," I told them. "I know money is really tight for you guys, but, your family's safety has to come first. I'll help you if I can."

"Thanks Dusty," Beth said. "I'm sure we'll be fine. But you know if we need you for anything, we won't hesitate to ask."

"I hope so Beth, I do mean it," I responded.

Emily's crying turned to occasional sobs as she lay belly down on the couch next to her mother. Beth's niece went into the kitchen and returned with the Children's Tylenol and handed it to Beth. Beth carefully measured out the thick liquid and gently tipped Emily's head up so she could swallow it. Emily went to put her head back onto the couch but then she stopped, staring at the front door. She began to cry again. We all looked at one another then to the front door. We neither saw nor heard a thing. Emily sat up, climbed into Beth's lap and clung to her, still crying. The phone rang and Edd picked it up and began speaking with Beth's mom again. As he wrote down flight information and was talking with her we heard pounding begin on the front door. It sounded like someone was trying to urgently get our attention. It wasn't a normal knock. The knocking ran up and down the center of the wooden door. It was hard and loud. We heard Edd tell his mother-in-law to hang on for a minute, he needed to answer the door. I was petrified. I couldn't move off the floor. I held my breath as Edd turned the doorknob.

"If that's you Steve, you're a dead man," Edd said as he swung the front door open as fast as he could.

We all expected one of Edd's drunk friends to be standing there when the door opened, but as soon as it swung open the heavy knocking sound stopped. There was no one there and the storm door was closed tight. Edd opened the storm door and ran out into the front yard. We could hear Edd yelling in the front yard.

"Stop it, stop it right now," he shouted into the night. "You're tearing my family apart and I won't have it anymore. You want to scare someone? You want to hurt someone? Bring it on you fuckers! I'm ready! You'll fuck with a baby and a pregnant woman, now try me! I'll fight you! Bring it on!" Edd screamed at the top of the roof where he said he'd seen Mud Man in the past.

I opened the storm door and said, "Edd? Your mother in law is still on the phone. I know you're pissed, but let's get Beth and Emily out of here first."

"You're right Dusty," he replied. "I'm just so mad at these sons of bitches. Let them come down here and mess with me for a change. I'll give them a run for their money." Edd returned into the house and his phone call.

"Come on Beth, let's get you and Emily packed for your trip," I said.

I accompanied Beth into Emily's room as she packed up as much as she could think of to bring.

"I have no idea how long we'll be gone," she said.

"Over-pack, Beth," I suggested. "I always do. If you wind up only being gone a couple of days don't worry about it. You know what I mean."

"Yeah I know what you mean," she said. "I still wish I knew why this was happening to us Dusty. But I guess we may never really know." Beth grabbed more of Emily's clothes and toys. I didn't bother responding because I had no answers for her. I wish more than anything else I did, but I did not. It was disheartening.

Beth stuffed as much as she could into the diaper bag and suitcase and I took them out to the living room while she started to pack her own things. I met her back in her bedroom and saw she was crying again. I tried to console her, but it was no use. I knew she wouldn't feel any better until she felt safe. And that may never happen again.

Edd appeared in their bedroom doorway and said, "Come on Mama, your plane leaves in two hours and I need to drop your niece off on the way to the airport. Get your stuff and let's get you two outta here."

"I'm almost done Edd," Beth replied.

"Do you want me to go with you Edd, to the airport I mean?" I asked.

"No Dusty. Thanks, but I need to be alone with Beth for a while before she leaves," he answered.

"I understand Edd," I replied. "Give me a call tomorrow and let me know what's going on. If you can find a place to stay other than here, please do so. I'll keep my ear out for houses for rent and you keep me posted daily."

"Will do, kiddo," he said.

"Beth, it's almost over," I told her. "When you get to your Mom's, let her take care of you and Emily so you can relax and get some rest. And call me if you need me."

"Thanks Dusty, I will," Beth said.

As I drove away from the Dunnam home that night I felt like I was in shock. So much had transpired that night it was unexplainable. If I had told anyone what I'd witnessed that night I would have been caught in a large butterfly net and taken off to be observed for a very long time. I ran through every detail in my head again and again, trying to rationalize what had happened, trying to find a sane explanation for the events that had taken place. I couldn't. I couldn't imagine what it was like to live in that house day in and day out for nearly a year with all that was going on. How could they have gotten so used to a situation that was so frightening? I realized I must have been in at least mild shock when I discovered I had passed my own street three times.

As I went in my front door I found Kyle asleep on our couch. I assumed he had tried waiting up for his crazy mother and as usual, she had been gone longer than his stamina would allow. I bent over and gave him a kiss on his forehead then sat down next to him and stared at him for what seemed like hours. I rubbed his back and wondered what I would do if the events of the Dunnam house ever occurred in my own home. My son was a good deal older than Emily, but still a child. I knew then the most important thing I could ever do when leaving a research site would be to tell the spirits to not follow me home. I wondered if I would ever get over the guilt I felt about Emily being attacked.

I checked my email just in case Edd had written before they left for the airport and found none from him. I wrote a quick note to him with the subject line of, "Want some Company?" I asked that if he wanted us to come and spend the night with him, all he had to do was ask. I felt it was the least I could do for him until he got moved into another house. I finished up my nighttime routine then grabbed a pillow and blanket and curled up on the floor next to the couch where my son slept. I felt a strong need to be as close to him as I could.

Chapter Eleven:
What More Could We Experience? Or Did We Really Want to Know?

I woke the next morning to find my son snuggling up against me while he watched cartoons. As soon as I opened my eyes he knew I was awake.

"Morning Mom," he said with a huge smile on his face. "Good Morning Bud! Sorry I was out so late last night. Did you try to wait up for me?" I asked.

"It's okay Mom," Kyle asked. "I know you were helping those people. I did try to stay up; you're not mad that I fell asleep on the couch are you?"

"No! No way! I'm glad you tried to wait up for me, just don't do it on school nights," I added with a laugh.

"Want me to make you some coffee," he asked.

"That would be very nice Kyle," I replied. "Thank you."

Kyle went into the kitchen and I tried to get my old tired and sore ass up off the living room floor. It really is terrible getting old. If I would have known in my youth how painful arthritis is, I would have protected my body better.

After working out the kinks I went through my morning routine and headed off to check my emails. I was hoping to hear from Edd about getting Beth and Emily onto the plane safely. I fired up the hamster-driven 246 and waited for it to get up to speed. I signed onto AOL under our research group's account which Edd always used to email me and found no email from him. I didn't bother to check any of my other screen names because Edd and Beth didn't know what they were.

I finished reading my DBPRGcontact@aol.com email and switched over to another screen name to read the 27 emails I found there. This was my personal account where I would get email from friends, relatives and my students. Kyle brought me a nice hot cup of coffee just as I was finishing the emails to that screen name. I noticed I had one email in the tours Inbox so I switched to hauntsofdaytona@aol.com expecting to find an email from a future tour guest. This would not be the case!

The return email address was Edd's business account, also on AOL. I noticed myself crinkling my eyebrows together in disbelief. Edd, who is not computer literate at all, was writing to me at an email address I didn't think he even knew about. I never told either of them the tour had a separate email address. It was also not listed on any of my advertising yet because I was unsure of how the tours would do. Below is a transcript of the email I received that morning:

Subj: Re: want some compny
Date: 1/10/2002 09:27:03 p.m. Eastern Standard Time
From: DunnamXXXXXXXXXX
To: HauntsOfDaytona

Thi is wireird.ther is a challenered.my hiar is up standing on end Emme has beuen freeid…

ed

My blood ran cold as I read the email. First, I noticed was the email came to an email address I was sure Edd and Beth knew nothing about. Second, the subject line had changed. It was a slight change, but a change all the same. I had written, "Want some Company?" The subject line's Reply read, "want some compny." The "W" and "C" were no longer capitalized, "company" was misspelled and the question mark at the end of the subject line was missing. Of course all of these things could be explained away. If Edd or Beth had found out about the other email address, it was possible for one of them to send an email to it and just type in everything, including "Re:" into the subject line. As Edd was not known for proper spelling or grammar, the misspelled word and incorrect punctuation could easily be explained away as well.

The third thing I noticed was the date and time: Jan. 10, 2002 at 9:27 p.m. We were still on the tour at that specific date and time! Could Beth's niece somehow have gotten the other email address and sent me an email? Possible, but unlikely, I concluded. Then I looked again to the subject line. I hadn't even written my email to Edd with that subject line until Jan. 11, 2002 at 2:15 a.m. How would any of them be able to respond with almost the same subject line, "almost" only because of spelling and punctuation mistakes, that I hadn't even written yet? This was way too weird for me, especially without even one full cup of coffee in me yet.

The next thing I noticed was the content of the email. Edd is a bad speller, but this stuff was unreadable in spots. The statement, "ther is a challenered" I stared at for several minutes and the only thing I could come up with was, "there is a challenge"? Or maybe even "there is a challenger?" After all Edd had challenged whatever was knocking on the front door that night. As for his hair standing up on end, Edd always had a crew cut, not enough hair to stand on end I thought to myself. But the part that really made my blood run cold was the statement of, "Emme has beuen freeid…" Who knew at 9:27 p.m. on Jan. 10, 2002 Emily would leave that terrifying house and be free of the nightmare she had been in for nearly a year?

The last thing I noticed was the signature. Edd was very adamant people knew he used two Ds in his name. The first night I had met him he had corrected all of my paperwork which used single Ds. This email was signed, "ed," with only one "D." Edd didn't strike me as the kind of guy who would formulate an intricate plan to use less Ds in his name to throw someone off the track of an email eight months into a paranormal investigation.

The most horrible thought of all suddenly popped into my still slightly, fuzzy brain. Could the entities at the Dunnam house send me an email? Was this possible? I know they can turn on lights, appliances, battery operated devices and move objects, even very heavy ones like golf clubs, but to write and send an email? I thought I would have to call Edd and ask him if I could stop by. I wouldn't tell him about the email so I could have a chance to look at his computer to see if it had been sent from there. I relied on Edd's limited computer skills to be unable to completely cover his tracks if the email had indeed been sent by someone in the house, other than the "ghosties."

I printed out the email and when Ros came in I showed it to her to get her opinion. I didn't share my thoughts.

"Dude, you got this email this morning?" Ros asked.

"Yep, just read it and printed it out before you came in," I answered.

"Man, how could Edd or Beth send it?" she asked. "They were on the tour with us at that time. Is there a way to send a, well, a time released email message?"

"Not that I'm aware of," I replied.

"Have you thought that maybe the 'ghosties' at Edd's house emailed you?"

"Oh my God, Ros," I exclaimed. "I was just sitting here thinking that very thing. Do you think it's possible?"

"Why not Dude," she replied. "We've seen, heard, and experienced some pretty strange shit in the past. Why couldn't they send an email? Although, they need to learn about the spell check button," she added, laughing.

I laughed with Ros and began to feel somewhat amused I may

have just received an email from a ghost. It was the first time I had ever heard of it, but then we had a lot of firsts happen to us on the Dunnam case. I showed the email to several people over the next couple of hours while trying to get a hold of Edd on the phone. Everyone I showed it to noticed the same things I did and questioned its origins. The general consensus was it may indeed have been sent by the ghosts. My mind and spirit now struggled with the facts. On the one hand, I hoped it had been Beth's niece that sent the email, but on the other hand I was thrilled that a ghost may have truly sent it.

It took several attempts to finally reach Edd on the phone. We were back to playing the phone game with the ghosts being in the middle, taking on the role of Ma Bell. "Edd?" I said as he picked up the phone. I wasn't sure at first that it was him as there was so much static on the line.

"Hey kiddo, what's up," he replied.

"Just checking in on you," I said. "Did Beth and Emme make it off okay?"

"Yeah, they got to her Mom's at about 4:30 this morning."

"That's good. Did you get much sleep?" I asked.

"Hell no," he exclaimed. "Fuckers had me up all night with their bullshit games; banging, pounding, throwing Emme's toys, scaring the crap out of Little Eddy. It was really a friggin' madhouse in here last night, Dusty, a real madhouse."

"Shit Edd! Why didn't you call me?" I asked.

"For what, so you could be kept up all night being annoyed by these fuckers too?"

"Well, at least you wouldn't have been there alone Edd."

"I appreciated it kiddo, but I think I needed to be alone with them last night and give them a challenge," he replied. "There was no way I was gonna let them scare me out of my own house."

There was the word, "challenge." He said that word to them out loud and they heard him. The time frame of the email still didn't make any sense, but the words did. I still didn't tell Edd about the email, I needed an excuse to go to the house to have a look at the computer before I could fill him in on what had happened.

"Mind if a couple of us stop by tonight Edd?" I asked.

"Not at all," Edd replied. "That would be great. After last night's fun activities I sure could use the moral support if nothing else."

"Did you burn the incense and candles last night, Edd?" I asked.

"No, I don't know where Beth put them," he replied. "She may have taken them with her by mistake. I'll stop at the store today and grab some more."

"Good. I want you to keep up with the routine every night."

"Sure thing, kiddo," he said. "Not a problem at all. See you guys tonight."

As soon as I hung up, I gathered the things for what could be another long night at the Dunnam house. I packed the bare minimum of equipment, but included as much of the cleansing items as my overnight bag would hold. I asked Ros to join me and called George to see if he could come as well. They both agreed.

We arrived at the Dunnam home right at 8:00 p.m. The front door was open with the storm door closed. I could see Edd standing at the kitchen bar talking on the phone. He motioned us to come in. I went straight to his computer and began searching for the email's trail. I checked the recently sent and recently deleted mail folders, the filing cabinet, the cache folders, the user folders, and the organize folders in all of the screen names. I found no email had been sent from any screen name on that computer on Jan. 10, 2002 at 9:27 p.m. I found all the previous emails they had sent me and I had sent them. I also found one Edd had sent only an hour ago seeking the type of incense to purchase, but no email from the previous night!

I could see Edd's reflection in the monitor as I searched his computer and he had a quizzical look on his face. I assumed he was speaking with Beth and I knew he was as soon as they began to discuss where she may have left the incense and candles. He finally hung up the phone and asked me what I was doing on his computer. I showed him a copy of the email. He looked it over carefully and his only comment was, "Who sent you this? That's not how I spell my name."

"I know Edd," I replied. "I'm not sure who sent it, but it's looking more and more like your 'ghosties' sent it to me."

"Is that possible?" he asked. "Wait, what am I saying? After living here for almost a year, I'm sure it's possible. They screw with our computer all the time."

I went over all the other anomalies I and others noticed in the email. He agreed it may have been the ghosts that sent it. We both racked our brains to try to come up with another possible answer to this mystery, but every path seemed to lead straight to the "other side."

We sat at the computer contemplating the mysterious email while Ros and George occupied Little Eddy in the living room. The overhead lights flickered on and off, and then on and off again. Little Eddy ran to Edd's side and a knocking sound started on the wall behind the computer.

"George, go in the bathroom in the hall and see if you can find this knocking noise," I shouted over the sound.

"I'm on it hon," George said as he made his way into the hallway.

I went into the family room and opened the back door to see if I could find a source for the sounds. I unlocked the door, but it wouldn't open. I turned the knob and pulled, but it didn't open. "Let me out," I said aloud, and it immediately opened. I was hit in the face with a blast of icy cold air as I stepped outside. It was 65 degrees outside, but the cold air I felt was freezing.

I checked around the walls and doors but found no source for the knocking sounds. I hoped George was having better luck. I was still holding onto the small hope this whole situation was somehow explainable by naturally occurring or man-made sources. Boy was I wrong.

When I went back into the house I saw Ros and Edd were checking the wall with the EMF and the thermal scanner. Edd had turned the computer off and unplugged it yet the EMF was still reading greater than 5. The temperature fluctuated 10 to 30 degrees, but in almost pinpoint locations on the wall. Both pieces of equipment would fluctuate as the knocking fluctuated and along the trail of the sound.

Just then, George stuck his head in the room from the hallway. His face was pale, his eyes were wide and it looked as though his hair was drenched with sweat.

"I couldn't find a source for the knocking sound," he said with a monotone voice.

"Are you all right George?" I asked.

"Yeah, but I swear to you someone turned the shower on when I was in the bathroom looking for the noise," he replied. "I was following it along the wall; it sounded like it was inside the wall. When I got to the tub and pulled back the shower curtain, I noticed the showerhead was dripping. So I decided to try to turn it off in case that's where the sound was coming from and as soon as I tightened the handle, wham! It turned back on full blast and soaked me!"

"Jesus, are you sure you're all right?" I asked, alarmed.

"Yeah," he said, laughing, "feeling kind of stupid for not seeing that stunt coming. Then the bastards shut it off again. At least they know not to waste water."

George shook his head and stood there, dripping with a forlorn look on his face like a dog that had just been forced to take a bath. Ros got up and grabbed a clean, dry towel and handed it to him. I told everyone no one was to go anywhere in the house alone, even to the bathroom. I wanted us paired up all night. And we would be staying all night. There was no way I was going to leave Edd there alone, no matter how much military training he had.

I asked Edd to get the incense and light some in the living room area. I grabbed two white candles and lit them as I recited St. Michael's prayer. I saw Edd place a black ashtray on the entertainment center and another on the kitchen bar. I moved a candle to each of these locations and when I set the one down on top of the entertainment center, I noticed the incense had a strange odor to it.

"Edd, is this the incense that I left here for you and Beth?" I asked.

"Nope," he replied. "Beth took that with her to Maryland. I stopped at the 7-11 today and bought some there."

"7-11 carries frankincense and myrrh incense?" I asked.

"Um, well, no, they don't. I grabbed some that looked like it would smell good."

"Where's the package Edd?"

"Right there on the kitchen counter."

I picked up the package of incense and discovered Edd had purchased "Sex on the Beach" incense cones. I giggled to myself as I thought what an interesting change this must be for the ghosts. As I stood there I also noticed the cone he had lit in the kitchen was not burning, but the one in the living room was smoking like mad. I walked to the entertainment center and read the advertisement on the side of the ashtray Edd had used to burn the incense cone in. It read, "Bates Motel," obviously a souvenir they had gotten from Universal Studios in Orlando. I turned around to yell at Edd about the poor choices he made for the incense and fireproof container when the ashtray flew off and hit me on the back before landing on the Oriental rug. The carpet immediately began to smolder and we scrambled to put it out. You would have thought we were trying to put out an out of control forest fire as we watched the smoldering carpet catch fire. It spread across the rug quickly as we patted and stomped at the growing fire. Ros grabbed her bottle of water and threw it on the blaze. There was no fan on, but it seemed that this fire was feeding off oxygen created in a wind tunnel. It was amazing how quickly this rug caught fire, almost as if someone had put gas or lighter fluid on the rug. This was crazy.

Edd called the next-door neighbor to find out if he and Little Eddy could stay with them until he found a new house. He would only need a place to lay his head at night for about a week or so, he said. They agreed Edd and the puppy could stay with them until Edd could secure another house. I felt great relief that Edd would not be alone in this house at night. I could see the relief on his face as well. My only fear was the ghosties might figure out where Edd had gone and would follow him. I tried not to focus on this.

Although we hadn't planned to spend the entire night with Edd, we decided since none of us had to be anywhere early the next morning we would stay and document any paranormal activity as this may be the last time we might ever visit the Dunnam home.

None of us got any sleep that night, except for Edd. He had fallen asleep in his easy chair and never moved until dawn. I guessed it was because he knew we were there and he would be safe. The rest of us stayed awake listening and documenting as much as we could. Doors creaked open and slammed shut. Lights, the television, fans and radios turned on and off by themselves. The "bodies being dragged across the floor" sounds came from the Florida room. Banging and knocking sounds and voices seemed to come from every corner of the house. The cats and Little Eddy would watch the unseen guests "walking" through the living room, and twice when Little Eddy tried to get a bite to eat, he ran whimpering back into the living room apparently scared to death.

On one of my walk-throughs, I noticed the closet door in Emily's room had been opened slightly and a couple of her toys, a small stuffed animal lamb and a boating life-preserver were in the middle of the bedroom floor. I knew from our previous documentation both of these items had been sitting on the top shelf in Emily's bedroom closet. It struck me as odd that these items had been chosen by the entities to be placed in plain sight, the innocent lamb and the life saving device. I dared not let my mind wander into the dark place it could have gone to. Emily and Beth were gone from this nightmare and, at least for now, were safe.

At 5:00 a.m. I lay down on the living room floor to cuddle Little Eddy. I gave him a fistful of puppy chow and he finally fell asleep. I listened for the rest of the night to someone walking up and down in front of the window by my head. I faced the window and watched intently hoping I would see a neighbor searching for a stray cat or maybe even a lawn man trimming the shrubs, but no such animal was there.

The footsteps crunched hard in the leaves and kept an even and steady pace for over an hour. I finally began counting them. Starting at the front door and going to the garage there would be twelve heavy footsteps. It was nearly 30 feet to cover that distance and I wondered if it was Mud Man looking for a way to get past the protection barriers we had put up; just one more thing to make my blood to run cold at the Dunnam house.

Edd woke up as his old self, cramming M&M's down his gullet and chugging a hot cup of coffee. He seemed to be feeling better or maybe it was just that he had gotten a decent night's sleep. He went through his morning routine in a quite chipper and jovial mood. It was really nice to see the Edd Dunnam I had met only eight short months ago.

Ros, George and I tried our best to be alert for the ride back to Daytona. I made Edd promise to call me at least once a day even if nothing happened. Also, if he needed to call more often or if anything did happen, I wanted a phone call immediately. He agreed and gave me the neighbor's phone number. He told me that the only thing he would be doing all day was searching for another place to live.

I hugged him good-bye, knowing that I would see Edd again, but instinctively knowing I would never step foot in this house again. I felt a sense of loss and relief at the same time.

We drove away from the Dunnam home not speaking, not knowing what the future would hold for the Dunnam family. I knew in my heart it would take me a long time to forget, if I ever could, the events I had witnessed and participated in that house. As I held that thought in my head my ribs began to ache reminding me of all the things that had occurred during the past several months. I knew I never wanted to work another case like this one. Even if one presented itself it would take a lot of convincing to get me to take it on. But I also realized the Daytona Beach Paranormal Research Group, Inc. was the only paranormal group in the area that had experience in dealing with nasty ghosts, I wouldn't be able to walk away from another family living with that level of fear in their own home.

Chapter Twelve:
The End of the Case,
Such as it was.

As he promised Edd called me every day to let me know how things were going. His first two days were hectic, but he was staying focused on the task of finding a safe home for his family. The third night however, things were different. He said he had decided to stay at his house instead of next door. That night, someone stole his work van with all of his tools inside of it and of course, he had left his wallet in the glove compartment. It turned out to be a real mess but the one good thing that came of it was Edd never spent another night in that house. The van and most of his tools were recovered a short time later.

It took Edd only nine days to find a new home. He didn't bring Emily and Beth home from Maryland until he had moved all of their belongings and bought a new crib for Emily. The new house was further south into the Orlando area and seemed to be perfect for them. Three bedrooms with two bathrooms, a nice garage and a big fenced in back yard for Little Eddy. The owner was willing to let Edd do remodeling work on the property in exchange for monthly rent. The only catch was the elderly woman who had been living in the house had passed away there and some of her personal items were stored in the garage. It sounded way too much like the situation they had just left.

I asked Edd why he had agreed to move into a similar situation and his response was a very simple one, "Well kiddo, not only do I feel that the lady who died there is not threatening, but if she were ever to become so, I have the knowledge, experience and friends to help me get a handle on the situation faster than the last time. Believe me, kiddo. I won't let things get out of control ever again. I realize now how much I have to loose."

It may seem crazy, but I understood what he meant and how he felt. I truly believe Edd Dunnam has the psychic gift of being able to see and hear entities and quite possibly, so does his daughter Emily. Because of this gift, I feel Edd would know if there were any entities in an area that could be a threat to his family. After living in the house on Hancock Road for nearly a full year, I was sure he would never allow them to go through anything even remotely akin to that again.

Edd continued to call at least once a day while he packed his belongings into boxes and made plans for his family to start over in the new house. He said the Hancock Road landlord was not pleased the Dunnam family had chosen to break their lease and leave almost a month early. Edd forcefully explained to the gentleman what had been going on and that if he tried to collect the last month's rent, Edd would bill him for all future therapy he and his family would need. It got pretty ugly and I repeated my offer to assist if he did take the Dunnam's to court. I would be there with all of the documentation to demonstrate he had rented the house to the young family knowing there were strange things, even potentially harmful things, going on in that house and he had denied it when asked about it. Edd said that seemed to shut him up pretty quick.

The very day that Edd was bringing his family home to their new house I received an email from Kelly Weaver. Although the case was over, her information was still very useful and confirmed our suspicions about several things in that house. The letter read:

Hi Dusty,

I am writing about the photos you mailed me. It took so long, because every time I went to touch them, I got a headache. Yuck! I finally made myself work on them this past Thursday. Sorry for the delay. Nasty stuff.

Here is my "read" on it.

HATE THE HALLWAY. I sense a man with major control issues. There is also a sad lost woman who walks around. I believe this home is surrounded by ley lines which "invites" a lot of things to pass through it. The feeling of being watched especially around the doors by the hallway. Again, don't like that place at all.

I see/feel loud bangs, the doors opening and shutting. I perceive the animals (if any) of the people who live there getting ill a lot. Unexplained illnesses.

The anger and tension that can be felt in this place can "blow the roof off."

Around the roof area, underneath is VERY powerful. This place is a "cesspool" of energy and it is not the nice kind. I would have a priest come and close the portal if possible.

I'll mail the photos back to you today. So sorry for the delay.

Best wishes.
Kelly Weaver

I emailed Kelly back and apologized for causing her such pain with this case. I know the type of headaches a psychic can get from a place that exudes negative energy and they make a migraine look like child's play.

I thanked her too for her accuracy. We all hated the hallway and it and the peak of the roof did seem to be where most of the activity centered. We knew of the older lost woman and the controlling "male" Mud Man figure. All of us had the feeling of being watched on many, many occasions. We had all also heard, seen or otherwise experienced the loud bangs, doors opening and shutting and an "anger" in that house. The only part that didn't make much sense in her email was animals having frequent and possibly unexplained illnesses. I later spoke with Beth and discovered they had lost several pets in their short stay in the home to unusual illnesses and one of the cats was always pregnant. Cats generally can have a litter of kittens once or sometimes twice a year, but the Dunnam cat had four litters in one year!

I have emailed a few times with Kelly and to this day I still thank her for assisting us with the Dunnam house case. She will never know how much relief I felt to know her perceptions were "right on" with what we had documented. I also will never forget the assistance and guidance given by Troy Taylor and Dave Juliano, nor will I forget the fact that Dave Osteen never bothered to even return an email.

We eventually did wind up doing an investigation at the new house, which did have some mild to moderate paranormal activity, more for Beth than anyone else. Her fear factor level was still so high from the other house that she wanted to know how "bad" the activity in the new house was.

The activity in the new house was so much different than that of the old house. We caught an orb coming down the hallway and going out the front door several times. We assumed this could be the elderly woman leaving her home as she did when she was alive. Otherwise, we noted a few orbs here and there and one unexplainable cold spot. Beth kept incense and candles burning all the time in their new home and it seemed to ease her fears.

Edd and Beth and I stayed in touch regularly for nearly two years after they moved. I lost touch with them when they had bought another house and moved further south. It's strange how a little distance can all but end a friendship; life just gets in the way. I think of them often and still have occasional nightmares about my experiences in that house. I often think of Emme and hope she was young enough to suppress those horrible occurrences. If not, she will make some therapist quite wealthy recounting her experiences. I wonder too if the newest member of the Dunnam family will possess the same abilities as his father and sister. For his sake, I sure hope not. After all, ignorance is bliss and no case proved that to me more than the year in hell; the haunting at the Dunnam house.

Dunnam House Floor Plan:

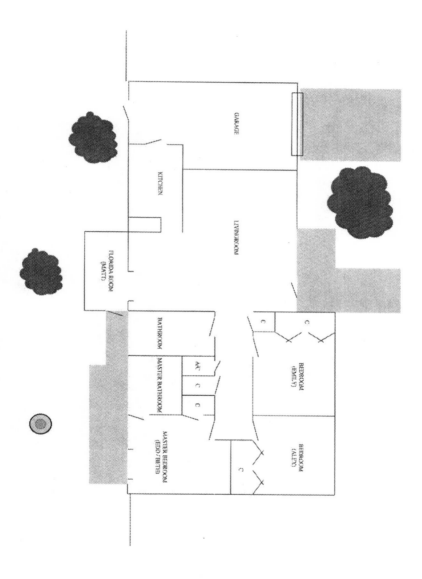

Epilogue:

I hope that you enjoyed this book. It took me nearly three years to write it all down. The facts in this book are true, only a couple of names were changed at the request of the person.

Should you say to yourself, "this book was boring;" I say, "come spend a night with me on Hancock Road." I checked on the house for over a year after Edd and Beth moved out. For the first four months it sat basically empty, the landlord couldn't seem to keep anyone in there more than a day or two. He finally rented it to a young couple with two small children and they stayed for about three months before fleeing in the middle of the night. They subsequently sued the landlord because their youngest child nearly lost an eye when a candleholder flew across the living room and struck him. The landlord finally sold the property last I heard, and the plan was to knock down the existing house. But that's only what I heard. I stopped driving by after a while because I found myself holding onto the feelings of guilt and helplessness. I needed to move on.

My cousins Cindy Lebow and Roger Scott, designer of the book's cover, and I drove by the house one final time in November 2004. As soon as we pulled up to the front of the house we all felt a heaviness in the air. It was unsettling to all of us, but what was more unsettling was to see a young couple with their two small children standing in front of the living room window decorating their Christmas tree. My heart sank as we watched and I hoped beyond hope that whatever had been in that home had gone on to another place or plane.

I learned a lot of valuable lessons in that house and I think that is the only thing I thank those entities for.

I wrote this book because I needed to get the facts out of my head so others might learn from our experiences and hopefully benefit from them. I know we made some mistakes during the case and I know we gained a lot of experience from it. I did not set out to write the *Amityville Horror* of the new millennium. The Dunnam family suffered greatly; emotionally, financially, and physically during their year in that house and I hope they can eventually put the experiences behind them. I only want the world to know that things that go bump in the night may not be always be your imagination.

Printed in the United States
82821LV00005B/34/A